ST. THÉRÈSE AND THE FAITHFUL

SAINT THÉRÈSE AND THE FAITHFUL

A BOOK FOR THOSE LIVING IN THE WORLD

by

BENEDICT WILLIAMSON

MEDIATRIX PRESS

MMXIV

ISBN: 978-0692320167

𝔑𝔦𝔥𝔦𝔩 𝔒𝔟𝔰𝔱𝔞𝔱:
C. SCHUT, S.Th.D.,
Censor deputatus.

𝔍𝔪𝔭𝔯𝔦𝔪𝔞𝔱𝔲𝔯:
✠ JOSEPH BUTT,
Vicar. Capitular.

WESTMONASTERII,
die 18 Februarii, 1935.

Mediatrix Press
607 E. 6th Ave.
Post Falls, ID 83854

TABLE OF CONTENTS

✧❦✧

DEDICATED TO
THE DISCIPLES OF
ST. THÉRÈSE OF LISIEUX

FOREWORD

I N writing this volume I had more especially in mind that large number of the Faithful who are enrolled in the Pious Union of the Disciples of St. Thérèse which has its centre at Lisieux; but it is also intended for all those who are striving to follow 'the little way' of love and confidence which the holy virgin of Lisieux has taught by word and example.

A chain is no stronger than its weakest link, hence the only true Christian social renewal must begin with the sanctification of each individual soul; as the spirit of love and sacrifice increases in individual souls so does the same spirit increase in the whole Church of God.

The Church is a living organism composed of a vast multitude of souls; just as our body is composed of a vast multitude of cells. In our body each cell lives its individual life in the life of the body, and the health of the body depends on the health of each separate cell. Thus it is in the Church the spiritual health of her body depends upon the spiritual health of each individual soul composing it.

The apostolate of our Saint is directed to the attainment of this personal spiritual renewal of each soul in the Church, and through it the renewal of the whole body. This relation between the individual soul-life and the collective life of the whole Church must always be kept in mind.

It is true as Marquis Albert de Pourvourville has said that the united voice of a praying multitude creates a favourable atmosphere for the outpouring of grace in abundant measure, and God Himself has attached a special promise to collective prayer, but the collective prayer is only efficacious to the extent that those who offer it have themselves first been quickened by the Spirit of God.

1

ST. THÉRÈSE AND THE FAITHFUL

As prayer ascending from a multitude has special power to touch the Heart of God, so likewise has prayer offered in special places. Hence pilgrimages such as those to Lourdes, Lisieux and many other places. Such places sanctified by the prayers and tears of vast numbers of souls seem, so to say, to be saturated with the supernatural, hence I hope that many of my readers may be enabled to take the pilgrim way to Lisieux.

I trust that the Disciples of St. Thérèse, for whom this book has been primarily written, may find in it a useful manual setting forth her doctrine and showing its application to the actualities of daily life. May it encourage and inspire them in the conflict which they must wage till death against the world, the flesh and the Devil, and above all help them to walk with assured confidence along the little way of love and *abandon* which their holy little Mistress sets before them.

BENEDICT WILLIAMSON.
ROME,
Feast of St. Thérèse of Lisieux, 1934

SAINT THÉRÈSE AND THE FAITHFUL

CHAPTER I
THE SECRET OF HER UNIVERSAL APOSTOLATE

HAT is the secret of the world-wide influence of St. Thérèse of Lisieux, of that Apostolate which has embraced every land and every clime, every people and every race, every class and state of life? An apostolate which not only embraces the children of the Church, but reaches out beyond and exercises the most astonishing influences over Orthodox, Protestants, Jews and Mohammedans? The Virgin of Lisieux appeals to all without exception; bishops, priests, religious, faithful, learned, unlearned, high and low, rich and poor, all alike come under the power of her influence.

It is less than forty years since our beloved little Mistress sped from the Carmel of Lisieux to the glory of Heaven. Of her brief earthly life of twenty four years, the last nine were lived within the walls of Carmel in so hidden a way, that even some of those living beside her were unaware that a saint was in the midst of them. And her death was as hidden as her life; how amazed the people of her time would have been had they been told that it was not the kings, emperors and politicians who were destined to be remembered, but a humble little nun of Lisieux, whose death had passed as little noticed as her life. Now they are forgotten even by their own peoples, while the Virgin of Lisieux is held in honour all the world over.

To combat the swelling pride and arrogance of this

twentieth century, God has made choice of this young Virgin of Lisieux. He has chosen her to be our Leader in the fight for the faith, and following her we shall tread underfoot all the might of the adversary. And why her? Why her? Why has His choice fallen upon her? Because He has chosen the weak things of this world to confound the strong, yea the very things that are not, to bring to nought the things that are. And the Saint of Lisieux repeats the same thought herself when speaking of the graces God had bestowed upon her: "If, as seems to me impossible, You could find a soul weaker than mine, I feel You would delight in loading that soul with yet greater favours, provided she abandoned herself with entire confidence to your infinite mercy."

Mark well her whom God has chosen to be our Leader; one whose life was so hidden that a lay sister, speaking to another about her approaching death and the circular which is sent out on such occasions, could say: "Mother Prioress will be hard put to it to find something to say about our little sister, for she has never done anything worth mentioning." Yet it is she who is chosen for the most wonderful apostolate in the history of God's Church: "It is the Lord's doing, and it is marvellous in our eyes."

The secret of her universal appeal, the secret of her power over souls is found in this, she teaches a doctrine of life which brings sanctity within the reach of all. She has been raised up by God to be the mistress of the spiritual life in these last days, and she speaks "as one having authority" because God has given her authority to speak.

And, like her Divine Master, St. Thérèse began to do and to teach, she first practised in her own life that which she was afterwards to teach. Her words came white-hot from a heart on fire with love of God, from a heart which had put to the test

8

every word of her teaching; this is the secret, this the only explanation of her power and influence over souls. Her doctrine has the double quality which we find in all the works of God, profundity and simplicity; so profound that the wisest cannot fully fathom it, so simple that the humblest soul can apprehend it.

The keynote of her doctrine is love. With St. Thérèse it is love which leads to perfection, not perfection which leads to love. Love is the mightiest and most irresistible power in the world even in the natural order, how much more so in the supernatural. What will not a soul do for love, what dangers will she not face, what sufferings will she not endure, will she not even give life itself for the loved? Fear may paralyse a soul with fright, so chill her whole being as to make her like some petrified corpse, but it will never inspire to heroic deeds and generous self-sacrifice. This, then, is the essential characteristic of her doctrine: "You ask me for a means of reaching perfection," she says in a letter to her cousin Marie Guerin. "I know of one only — love. Let us love, for our heart was created for this alone." And she continues: "But upon whom shall your heart pour out its love? Who is great enough to receive its treasures? Can a human being comprehend it? And, above all, return it. There is but one Being who can comprehend our love — Our Jesus. He alone will return infinitely more than we can give."

At first sight there is a strange paradox running through all the teaching of our little Mistress; two thoughts always in juxtaposition and yet seemingly so contradictory: *Love* and *War*. She is the lover, flaming with love for her Heavenly Bridegroom, but she is also the eager warrior, prompt to battle for Him who is her King as well as her Spouse. She fights because she loves, and as she speaks of love in the same breath

9

she speaks of war. Listen to this:

> "Jesus, to You alone I cling,
> To Your arms I fly to hide.
> I would love You like a little child.
> I would fight for You like a valiant warrior.
> Like a child full of tenderness,
> Lord, would I load You with caresses
> And on the field of my apostolate
> Like a warrior fling myself into the fight."

or this:

> "My peace, is to battle without respite."

or again, in one of her last verses:

> "Smiling would I face the fire
> And in Your arms, my Spouse divine,
> Would sing as on the battlefield I die. *Arms in hand!*"

St. Thérèse well understood the twofold character of our life down here, Love and Combat, and realized to the full in her own life the truth that these two are inseparable. In Heaven the war will be over and Love alone will remain. In *Patria* the soldier's life is finished; while the life of the lover endures everlastingly. We can only understand St. Thérèse in the light of her apostolate as a great teacher of the spiritual life. True, she has wrought more miracles than any other saint, but this is the accidental and not the essential side of her mission, the divine seal on the truth of her teaching; her real mission is to teach souls to love Jesus as she has loved Him.

And her teaching appeals to the most diverse souls, because hers is a doctrine of life, for the Catholic religion is only vital to the extent that is expressed in terms of life. True, it is a most marvellous system of theology, a remarkable organization, a wonderful philosophy, a most complete system of morality. Yes, it is all these, but above all it is a life, a life lived in the power of God, a life lived in the strength of the Holy Ghost, a life which transforms the whole being and brings it into subjection to the spirit. The essential task of the Catholic Church on earth is to gather together a multitude of souls who shall love God through all eternity. This is why the mission of St. Thérèse has such a universal application, this is why it has appealed to the most diverse races and peoples, because it puts before all a way of life, begun and perfected by love.

Look at the many religious Congregations bearing her name which have come into existence in the few years which have passed since she was raised to the highest honours of the altar! Look at the wonderful pilgrimage to Lisieux, one which impresses you with its quiet, penetrating reality, for these souls are all intensely earnest about the only thing which matters. Look at the austerely beautiful basilica which is rising on the hill above the city, austere, but surprisingly beautiful and still more surprisingly original that one almost seems to hear her saying: "I make all things new." All this is but part of the vast apostolate which she exercises throughout the world. Is not this the realization of her own prophecy: "I shall spend my heaven in doing good upon earth"?

Our little Mistress first felt the call to the apostolate for souls one Sunday, some two years after her first Communion, when, as she was closing her prayer book at the end of Mass,

11

a picture of the Crucifixion slipped partly out, showing the Blood flowing from the pierced hands of the Saviour, the sight of which set her soul aflame with zeal for the salvation of souls. She chose Carmel as the place whence to work because she felt the range of her apostolate would be wider than in an active order, for from that holy place she could, by prayer and sacrifice, embrace the whole world, and as the years of her cloistral life sped by God more and more clearly revealed to His chosen apostle the work she was to accomplish after her death.

More than once she gives expression to the feeling of constraint which she felt while yet in the flesh, and the assurance that it was only after her release from the body that her mission would begin. A few weeks before her death while looking at a picture of St. Jeanne d'Arc in prison she exclaimed:

"The Saints encourage me too, in my prison. They say to me: 'As long as you are in chains you cannot fulfil your mission, but a little later, after your death, then the time of your conquests will begin.'"

On July 17 in the same year she said to Mother Agnes: "I feel my mission is about to commence, *my mission of making souls love God as I have loved Him,* of teaching them my little way. If my desires are fulfilled I shall spend my heaven upon earth till the end of the world. *Yes, I shall spend my heaven in doing good upon earth.* That is not impossible seeing that from the midst of the Beatific Vision the angels watch over us. I shall not take my rest till the end of the world, so long as there are souls to be saved. When the angel shall declare that 'time shall be no more,' then I shall take my rest, then I shall rejoice, because the number of the elect will be complete, and all will have entered into their joy and their repose."

When Mother Agnes asked her for some explanation of

what she would teach after her death, she replied: "It is the way of confidence and total *abandon*. I would show them the little means which I have found so perfectly successful, and tell them there is but one thing to do down here: to throw Jesus the flowers of little sacrifices and win Him by caresses."

Speaking of a favour granted her earlier in the same year she said: "If a desire thus expressed is so fulfilled, it is impossible that all my great desires of which I speak constantly to God should not be completely realized," and in that last manifestation of her soul to her eldest sister Marie, she reveals again the immense range of those desires stretching forth through the ages to come till the day of doom, and embracing all the peoples and nations of the earth.

And to the question: "You will look down upon us?" she answered: "*No, I shall come down*," and in all parts of the world and in the most varied circumstances she has come down; to soldiers on the battle-front in the Great War, to people under all sorts of conditions, bringing consolation and healing for body and soul.

Two thousand years ago the Blessed Virgin of Nazareth as she sang her Magnificat uttered this amazing prophecy: "*Behold from henceforth all generations shall call me blessed.*" Absolutely unlikely of realization at the moment of its utterance that prophecy appeared, and yet through all the ages since it has been fulfilled to the letter, because: "God's words are deeds and do what they say."

Nigh two thousand years later the young virgin of Lisieux makes a prophecy scarcely less startling in its boldness, and seemingly as unlikely of fulfilment as that of the Immaculate Mother herself: "*Ah ! I know it well, all the world will love me!*" Words startling in their calm assurance, words which we see fulfilled before our eyes, for "All the world has gone after her," and some are inclined to repeat the words said of Our Saviour long ago: "Whence has this man all these things?" and say: "Whence has this young girl all these things?" She herself gives the answer: "I am too little to be vain, I am too little even to tell in fine phrases how great is my humility. I prefer to simply say *He that is mighty has wrought great things in me.*" The daring boldness of her prophecy springs from the realization of her own nothingness and of God's infinite greatness, and the assurance that He alone has bestowed all these things upon her.

Our holy Patroness calls us to follow her little way of love and complete *abandon* to God's Will. This implies a permanent disposition of soul by which we desire and seek nought *save* the perfect accomplishment of God's Will in ourselves and in others. The French word *abandon,* which is so expressive, has no equivalent in our English tongue, but we must try and realize what St. Thérèse means when she uses this word. It does not mean resignation, because this often means an unwilling submission to the inevitable, nor even a conformity to the Divine Will, but a loving, joyous and willing acceptance of it, no matter how great the sacrifice or suffering which it involves, the desire to exist solely in order to give pleasure to the Heart of God in all the varied circumstances of life.

As love grows in the soul, the spirit of *abandon* grows with it, for it is the precious fruit of love; a lover cannot bear the thought of any resistance to the will of the beloved, even in the natural order; so is it in the supernatural order, a soul in love with Jesus has only one desire, to please her Divine Lover to the fullest extent of her power.

Love changes the whole outlook on life. Without God's Will nothing can ever happen to me; absolutely nothing. His Almighty Power, His All Seeingness are under the guidance of

His Infinite Love, therefore, love it is which allows each happening to befall me from the first moment of my life until the last. Like our beloved little Mistress, we must seize every occasion which offers in order to throw our adorable Jesus the flowers of little sacrifices. And what does this mean? To hold back an angry retort when provoked, and make as if we had not heard it, to do a little act of kindness to one who has not been kind to us, to seize every opportunity which befalls us of bearing some little cross for love of our Jesus, even if sometimes to do so costs much, and our offering is not without tears. Jesus knows our weakness, and He will understand that even if the tears cannot be restrained we gladly make the sacrifice, even though our poor heart is almost broken at the giving.

These are our flowers of love and sacrifice! Thus it is that gradually one thought alone dominates our life; to seek in the daily round of work and duty to do all so as to give Jesus a little pleasure. To live as St. Thérèse expresses it, "in an act of perfect love." That is the "sure way" of our beloved Mistress, a way in which there is no danger of illusion, a way which the simplest and humblest soul may tread with assured confidence.

St. Thérèse calls upon souls to tread this path, to enter upon her "little way" which will lead right up to the gates of Heaven, and transform all their actions into pure gold, even the most insignificant, since each will be done in Jesus, with Jesus, and for His pleasure alone.

Of one thing I am very sure, once a soul has entered on this way she will enjoy a liberty of spirit and a happiness unknown before. The world over souls are treading this way of love, confidence and *abandon* which they have learned from the Virgin of Lisieux, but the heart of our little Patroness is still unsatisfied, she calls for more and more, and would enlist the whole world under her banner.

Love is the beginning and love the ending. We begin this little way in love, and we shall finish it in love. Love runs with eager haste to sacrifice everything for the sake of the Beloved. Love makes the impossible to be possible, overcomes every obstacle, breaks down every barrier, because nothing can resist love.

CHAPTER II
THE APOSTOLATE OF LOVE

HÉRÈSE, reflecting on all the possible vocations which could be hers, finally came to the vocation of love: "In considering the mystical Body of Holy Church I could not discover myself in any of the members described by St. Paul, or rather, I wished to see myself in all. Charity gave me the key to *my vocation.* I understood that as the Church is a body composed of different members, the most noble and the most necessary organ of all could not be lacking to her. I realized that she had a heart, and a heart aflame with love. I saw, too, that love alone moves all the members to action; so that if love should be extinguished, apostles would no longer preach the Gospel and martyrs would refuse to shed their blood. I realized that love embraces all vocations, that love is all, embraces all times and all places because it is eternal. Then in a delirium of joy I cried: 'O Jesus, my Love, I have found my vocation at last—my *vocation is love!* Yes, I have found my place in the womb of the Church, and this place, O my God, You Yourself have given me. *In the heart of the Church my Mother I shall be Love!'* Thus shall I be all things, thus shall my dream be realized."

This, then, is the apostolate of our beloved little Patroness and Leader, in the heart of God's Church she is the Apostle of Love.

"Without love," she writes, "our works even the most

brilliant count for nothing, Jesus does not demand great deeds, but only gratitude and *abandon,* that is to say, Love. . . . *God has no need of our works, but only of our love."*

Again: "It is not riches and glory, not even the glory of Heaven that my heart craves: what I ask is, Love!"

Love is the mightiest power in the universe, for nothing can resist it. For love men will do and dare anything. Love will face the most terrifying experience unafraid. This is true also in the natural order. A boy will risk his neck to get something for which the girl has a fancy, and the greater the danger the greater the pleasure in bringing the thing desired to the one he loves.

Love vanquishes every obstacle, attempts things which to the non-lover appear impossible, not only attempts but does them, because urged on to desperate endeavour by the compelling force of love; there is no limit to the sacrifice and heroism love will inspire. After all, it is the most Godlike quality in man, even in his natural state, for love, whether natural or supernatural, has its source in God, who *is* Love.

Can supernatural love equal at its highest natural love? A learned non-Catholic minister put this question to himself, and replied in the negative. But supernatural love not only equals but surpasses natural love even at its highest. Look at our little Patroness herself. She loved her father and sisters with the most intense affection, and yet calmly and quite deliberately she sacrificed all for the love of Jesus. He had claimed all and she would give all. The dominating, imperious, compelling love of Jesus had captivated her heart. But did that love of Jesus kill her natural love, dull her natural affection for those whom she loved? No, for she herself has declared that the heart given to God loses nothing of its natural tenderness; listen to her experience at the portal of Carmel when the moment of separation came: "Leading the way to the door of the cloister, my heart was beating so violently that I felt I must die. Ah, that moment, what anguish! One must have experienced it to understand it." Yes, the poor wounded heart suffered indeed, but did she hesitate? No, not for an instant, the supernatural love for the Divine Lover triumphed over all human love, and even though the parting seemed like death, our heroic little Mistress still went forward.

And this is verified again and again, for those whom the Divine Lover calls to make the supreme sacrifice are those whose hearts are the most tender and the most responsive to the touch of love. How can they make the sacrifice? How leave behind those they love so ardently? The Divine Lover has touched the heart, and for His Love all other loves must be fled.

Look at the martyrs and all the torments they endured. Look at the intrepid heroism of little Maria of Padua, one who in our own century reproduces the martyr spirit of the first. Here you see supernatural love at its highest, a love to which nothing is impossible. How often souls have been held back from sanctity by the paralysing doctrine of Jansenism, the remnants of which, even yet, remain, although the heresy has been cast out so long. How often spiritual books are written in a way which terrifies rather than encourages. Our little Mistress knew this well: "Sometimes in reading certain books of devotion, where the way of perfection is presented to us as beset with a thousand obstacles, my poor head is quickly fatigued. I shut the learned treatise which has tired my head and dried up my heart and take up the Holy Scriptures. Then all becomes clear, a single word opens to my soul infinite horizons, perfection appears easy, and I see it suffices to acknowledge my nothingness, and abandon myself like a child in the arms of God."

19

ST. Thérèse and the Faithful

As our beloved Leader has shown us the only way to true perfection is love, and as she has so well said, Jesus alone can satisfy our love, for He only can fully comprehend it. How often have we given our love to creatures only to find it either undervalued or misunderstood; or even despised. Our heart has only been created in order to love, that is its essential function, and although our heart is so small and insignificant, yet the love which it holds is so great that it can only be satisfied with the love of God Himself. Earthly love, however great, can never fully satisfy the hunger of our heart for a love that is Infinite.

It is not enough to love, we must be loved, and love returned in equal measure by the one loved. That is why earth is such a land of exile and sorrow. *Love gives all but it likewise demands all, and demands it very imperiously.* Only One there is who will return our love, not only adequately but superabundantly, infinitely, and that one is Jesus. *All* the infinite Love of Jesus can be mine, just as if I was the only being existing in all this vast universe. *All* His Love, not a part, but the whole. It seems incredible, impossible, but it is true. Look at the sun shining in the heavens, giving light and warmth to the earth! Suppose I was the sole being existing upon it, could I enjoy more light and heat than I do now, when millions of others enjoy the same gift? Does one take aught from the enjoyment of the other? No, each one of us enjoys all the light and heat of the sun. This is merely an illustration, and inadequate as all illustrations must be when dealing with the Infinite, yet it helps us to understand that each one of us in love with Jesus has *all* the love of Jesus as if the only creature in existence.

The secret of St. Thérèse is *Love;* for love is the secret of secrets. God Himself *is* Love, and all the natural love which we

20

behold upon earth, the love of father and mother for children, of sisters for sisters, brothers for brothers, lovers for lovers, husbands for wives, wives for husbands, of children for parents, love under whatsoever aspect we behold it, under whatsoever form it has existed in the past or shall exist in the future, all the love of the whole human race from the day of creation till the day of doom is only a feeble reflection of the Infinite Love of God from whose Heart it all draws its origin. Yes, in giving our heart's love to Jesus we shall never be disappointed. All things around may change and fail, all our hopes and desires be disappointed, but His Love will never fail, and never disappoint us. If only we would turn the love we so vainly lavish upon creatures to Jesus, what a transformation it would effect in our lives. Indeed, so great would be the change that we should seem to live in another world. Earthly love is unstable, uncertain. How often we have been deceived, how often we have felt that at last we have met a love strong as death, or stronger, then the moment of disillusionment has come, and we have experienced all the bitterness of discovering the uncertainty of human affection and the little reliance we can place upon it.

Like our little Teacher, we must put the love of Jesus in the first place. Love Him for Himself alone, love Him intensely, passionately, as if there was none other to love in the whole universe: *Jesus must be our first love and our last.* We must give Him our heart, He must possess it, then we shall experience the sweetness and peace which comes from loving Him before all else in the whole world. Then we shall be transformed by the Living Presence of the Divine Lover in our heart.

The effect of this Divine Supernatural Love upon our whole life down to its smallest details will be amazing. Henceforth we shall only exist to please Jesus. As we toil at our work, humble, lowly and hidden though it be, our one thought will be that at each moment we are giving pleasure to Our Divine Lover.

What shall we think about? Where our heart is, there is our treasure also, so we shall think about Jesus, think of His immense love for us, how much He suffered for us, how He embraced every torment that has ever afflicted humankind and united it all together in the tremendous agony of the Cross. If you love anyone you find no difficulty in thinking about him, rather the difficulty is the other way, because you cannot stop thinking about him.

That is how we must be with Jesus, love Him so much that we cannot stop thinking about Him.

This thought will control our words, for we only want to speak so as to please Him. We shall hold back words which we know will displease. When provoked, instead of making an angry reply we shall keep silence. We shall never speak unkindly of anyone, never be hard on anyone, however bad they be, never speak harshly of their fall, however great it be, but try and find something good in them of which we may speak.

Then all the little crosses, trials and sufferings of life will wear a different aspect. We shall endure them gladly for love of Jesus. We cannot rejoice in pain, crosses, afflictions in themselves, but we can rejoice in them because they liken us to Him we love. *Love makes likeness.* The lover's one desire is to be like the beloved. Our one desire, then, is to be like Jesus. "When," says our little Teacher, "a soul is entirely given up to love, all her actions, even the most indifferent, are stamped with that divine seal." Yes, love sets its seal on all our actions, words and thoughts. The closer the soul draws to Jesus the more is she conformed to His Likeness.

The world can only come to know Jesus through His

lovers, hence we must be the manifestation of Jesus to all around us. We must so live, as says St. Paul, that Jesus Himself may be manifested in our mortal bodies, that men looking at us may see Jesus reflected in us. "To live of love," exclaims our holy Patroness, "is to give without measure and never lay claim to any reward down here. I know well that my only riches is to love always."

What a glorious apostolate we can exercise over the world by our life, so hidden and humble that the world heeds it not. Listen again to our little Mistress: "By our little acts of charity practised in secret we shall convert souls afar off, help the missionaries, obtain for them numerous gifts and so build spiritual and material habitations for Jesus."

The young servant girl working from morning till night at work which never seems to end, can be an apostle; as she scrubs, sweeps and toils she is converting sinners, sustaining missionaries in their labours, doing more for God than if she had the eloquence of St. John Chrysostom, and could preach to the whole world at once.

It is this hidden apostolate which really counts, for nothing can resist it. The young girl works, and offers all to Jesus for His pleasure and the salvation of souls. Thus love glorifies her humble task which becomes radiant in the light of love. She sees no fruit of her toil down here, but she will see its glorious result in Heaven, and receive the loving gratitude of the souls she has helped to save by her life of hidden sacrifice.

But what of human love? Is it utterly excluded by this overwhelming supernatural love of Jesus, is the soul so overwhelmed by it that she had no thought, no feeling for aught besides! No, supernatural love, far from destroying our natural love and affection, increases, deepens, above all, sanctifies it, and gives it that stability which only supernatural grace can impart. We love Jesus for Himself alone, but we love all others in Him and for Him. We love not less but more, because our love has a supernatural foundation. All whom Jesus loves, we love. Our love becomes wider, more universal, more all-embracing; more tender and affectionate as we increase in the love of Jesus. Seeing Jesus in all we love, in loving them we are loving Him. And our love is constant and unaffected by the variations in the one we love. We love as Jesus loves, love because He loves, and hence our love reflects something of the changelessness of God Himself.

Human love oftens fails, and life is full of tragedies because this love has no supernatural foundation to give it stability, hence the inconstancy of the affections, which so easily pass from one object to another. *But when we love in Jesus we love for ever.*

God has given us a head with which to know Him and a heart with which to love Him. We must know Him in order to love Him, but knowledge without love does not suffice. We may know a person very well and yet have no love for him. If there is to be intimacy there must be love. Two meet each other frequently perhaps, and know a great deal about each other, but they are merely acquaintances. Then one day comes that mysterious something like a flash of lightning, and the fire of the love burns in the heart of each: the distance which separates the moment before from the moment after is almost infinite. Before they did not love, now they do, and a whole world lies between the two. Of what avail is faith without love; it is as fire without heat. Our hearts were created for love and for love alone. Of what avail is immense learning or vast knowledge without love? How many failures in the spiritual life can be traced to this. Stars have fallen from the firmament of the Church, *they possessed every gift but one, and that the most essential of all, they had no love.* Yet they had hearts created for love like the heart of each one of us. Then came the crisis, when the heart rose up and claimed the satisfaction so long denied, and because it had not been satisfied with supernatural love, it sought satisfaction in the merely natural. Only one Lover can give our poor heart all it craves for, as our beloved Saint realized - and that Lover is Divine, Jesus Christ Himself.

Towards the end of 1896 our holy Patroness wrote: "Amongst the graces without number which I have received this year, I count as by no means the least the understanding which I received of the far reaching precept of charity. I had never before fathomed those words of Our Lord: 'The second commandment is like unto the first: You shall love your neighbour as yourself.' I had set myself above all to love God, and *it was in loving Him* that I discovered the secret of those other words: 'Not everyone who says to me Lord! Lord! shall enter the Kingdom, but he who does the will of my Father in Heaven!' That will Jesus revealed to me when, at the Last Supper, He gave *His new commandment* to His Apostles, telling them to love one another as He had loved them. I enquired how He had loved his Apostles; and I saw it was not for their natural qualities, for they were ignorant men, full of earthly ideas. Yet He called them His friends, His brethren, and will have them close to Himself in the Kingdom of His Father, and to open that Kingdom for them He will die upon the Cross saying: 'Greater love has no man than this, that he lay down his life for his friend.' As I reflected on these Divine words, I realized how imperfect my love for my sisters had been, for I saw I had not loved them as Jesus loved them. *Ah, now I know true love consists in bearing with all the defects of our neighbours, and never being surprised at their weaknesses, but rather in being delighted with the smallest of their virtues. . . .* In the Old Law when God commanded His people to love their neighbours as themselves, He had not yet come down upon earth. Knowing well to what a degree we go on loving ourselves, He would not ask anything greater. But Jesus came and gave His Apostles a new commandment — His own commandment. He not only requires us to love our neighbours as ourselves but to love them even as He has loved and will love till the consummation of the world. O Jesus, I know You never command the impossible. You know my frailty and imperfection far better than I know it myself. You know well that I shall never love my sisters as You love them, unless You Yourself come and love them *in me.* It is because You wish to give me this grace that You have given this *new* commandment. Oh, how I love it, since it enables me to love ... Yes, I know when I am loving others it is Jesus alone who acts in me; the more I am united to Him, the more dearly do I love *all* my sisters."

There you have a wonderful exposition of her doctrine of love in its relation to others. The source of her love for others comes from her love of God ; because she is in love with God she is also in love with all those around her, and she realizes that she can only love others as she ought, through the indwelling presence of Jesus, who loves them in and through her.

How completely this changes our attitude to others. We love them in spite of their defects and failures, in spite of the things which irritate us in them. We are never surprised at their failures and defects, and instead we are rejoiced and delighted at the smallest appearance of virtue. Once we have realized this we are full of sympathy and understanding for others, and we see how often their defects arise from their endeavours to do well.

How easy it is in the eager haste to give pleasure to Jesus to make some slip and fall just as the child who runs to its mother may trip and fall over some unseen obstacle because the child's eyes are fixed on the mother.

Love has this wonderful virtue that it transforms all it touches. Once we begin to love in this supernatural way we shall never be hard in our judgements of others. We can never be too merciful in our judgement of anyone, no matter how badly they may have acted. Instead, we shall be full of pity and compassion, eager to help them on to their feet again, at least, by our prayers, if we cannot do more, for prayer pierces every obstacle and melts the hardest heart.

It was by being sweet, gracious and gentle to the most difficult characters that our loving little Mistress won the hearts of all. Her gracious manner, her winning smile, her gentleness broke down every barrier. Sweetness, graciousness, gentleness, these are three distinguishing marks of the soul in love with Jesus in her dealing with others. See how supernatural love works and how it gradually changes the most hopeless natures; the rough, the ungracious, the hard, become sweet, gracious and gentle; this is the triumph of love.

What a difference a sweet smile makes, even when one has to say something rather hard to bear for the one who had to hear it. A rebuke given with sweetness always produces its effect while one given with severity generally produces the opposite result to that desired. So much depends upon the manner in which a thing is said or done.

A gracious manner of doing or saying, the unaffected gentleness with which it is accompanied, counts for so much. It is so easy to be rough and rude, so much more difficult to retain, no matter what the circumstances, a gentle, gracious manner. There is no merit in saying: "Oh, I just say what I think, I am blunt and outspoken," because it is only too painfully evident and needs no emphasis. Real merit comes in when being really hurt and wounded, even angered, we crush it all down and give a gentle answer and a sweet smile to the one who has provoked us.

True, it needs discipline and self-sacrifice to maintain this sweet gentle manner under all circumstances, but we must persevere. If at times we fail, let us tell Jesus at once that we are sorry, lose no time in useless regret, but begin again with renewed determination and finally a sweet gracious manner will become habitual with us. We must be particularly careful to show gentleness towards those in whom this quality is lacking. Then, just as the sun warms the coldest substance simply by shining, so we shall warm the coldest heart by the gracious sweetness of our behaviour.

How often we perform an act of kindness, and not only receive no thanks, but quite the reverse. If we listen to nature we shall say: "It will be a long day before I put myself out for that one again." But if Jesus is within us, we shall remember we did it not to receive thanks from creatures but solely to please Him, and as He is pleased, that is all that matters.

The life of love is a joyous life, even amidst crosses and tribulations the soul yet keeps her joy and peace, because she is not set upon the things that pass, but only desires to use each moment to give pleasure to her Lover. There is only one thing to do down here: to love Jesus and win souls for Him that so He may be loved. "Let us seize with jealous care even the smallest opportunity for self-sacrifice, let us refuse Him nothing - He does so want our love," thus wrote our beloved little Teacher to her sister Celine.

And on another occasion she remarks: "True love is

nourished by sacrifice," for she well realized that in time love manifests itself by sacrifice, and that where there is no sacrifice there is no love.

Love gives assurance even in the most stormy and difficult moments of life that despite appearances to the contrary, all is well, that He will make all to be well, and that all the sufferings and trials through which we are passing will surely bring a greater good, since *"All things* work together for good to those who love God."

Listen to these sweet and gracious words of our beloved Teacher: "O Jesus, I have no other means to prove my love for You than by throwing my flowers; that is, never letting pass unheeded any little opportunity for sacrifice, so that my smallest action may be wrought through love alone."

It is by her apostolate of love that our holy Patroness has captivated the hearts of all, so that in truth we can say: "Behold the whole world has gone after her."

CHAPTER III
THE APOSTOLATE OF WAR

AFTER, or rather along with, the apostolate of love comes the apostolate of war, for the one is inseparable from the other in the mind of our beloved Teacher. Her attitude towards war may be summed up in a single sentence: "I fight because I love," for the fire of love for her Heavenly Bridegroom urged her forward to fight for the triumph of His cause; it was love alone which gave her strength for battle. She realized to the full that our life upon earth is a warfare, that we belong to a kingdom which is mobilized for war, a kingdom in which all the citizens are soldiers. She faced the battle unafraid, a battle which she knew would only be over on the day of her death. But her soldier-spirit reached out beyond death, she would be the Leader in the warfare till the end of the world, only then when the number of God's elect was made up would she take her rest. One battle, one life of conflict was not enough for her, by her presence and spirit she would inspire and hearten all God's soldiers till the end of time.

Love and war, these two are united in the mind of our heroic little Leader; she cannot think of one without the other, for in this world the life of love means the life of warfare. One day some six months before her death when St. Thérèse was enduring intense suffering, for a few moments during prayer-time she fell asleep and dreamt there was a war on. " In my dream," she said to Mother Agnes, "it seemed there was a lack of soldiers for a war, and you said, we must send Sister Thérèse of the Child Jesus. I replied that I wished that it had been a holy war, but I set out all the same," then after a moment's reflection, with her face lit up with enthusiasm, she went on: "O Mother, what a joy it would have been to have fought at the time of the Crusades or later on against the heretics. I should not have feared the fire of battle. Is it possible that I shall die in bed?" This shows the spirit of our brave little Leader. Her spirit is that of the first century, when the fighting spirit of the Church was strong, and to die in bed was looked upon at least as a misfortune when one might have died gloriously in the arena. May she impart to us something of her dauntless spirit so that we may face the combat as courageously as she.

True, the war in which she and we are engaged is a spiritual war, but it *is* war all the same, one which calls for more desperate courage than any mere earthly conflict, because the things for which we fight are so immeasurably more precious. They fight for an earthly kingdom, we for a Heavenly. There is this difference between earthly and spiritual warfare. Earthly wars at the worst are over in a few years, but our war will continue as long as we live, and go on after we are dead. So there is no good in looking forward to a quiet time down here, because it will never come, we must fight till we die without thought of truce or armistice, fight on till, sword in hand, like our little Saint, we die upon the field of battle. A very favourite delusion of the Devil is that of trying to deceive the soul with the idea of finding a quiet corner somewhere in the world where there is no conflict and where, so to say, we may anticipate the peace of Heaven; a pitiful delusion indeed, for such a place never has, does not, and never will exist down here. As long as we are on earth we are soldiers in the battle-line who dare not relax our vigilance for a moment.

Of course, not all in the Kingdom have the true fighting spirit, there are feeble-kneed Catholics to whom the prolonged conflict is distasteful, and they would gladly come to a compromise with the world and the flesh, and make a truce with the Devil.

These feeble folk are as great a danger in the spiritual army as they would be in an earthly army, for they impart something of their own fears to those who otherwise would have fought courageously. No,

> "We want no cowards in our ranks
> Who will their colours fly,"

but only those who will bear themselves fearlessly and put to flight the armies of Hell. The Church is strong to the extent that the fighting spirit is strong in the hearts of her children, to the extent that they face world, flesh and Devil with the determination to triumph, be the cost what it may. For an army to be victorious, it must be confident, strong in the assurance that it can and will vanquish the foe: a discouraged, disheartened army is already beaten before the fight begins.

We have to fight against the world, the flesh and the Devil, these are our enemies, and we must fight against them till death ends the conflict, and in this strife we have the assurance that our beloved Leader will be with us, that her spirit will be present to strengthen us just when we need that strength the most.

First of all we have the world, not the earth, the sea and the sky, but the spirit by which those who are of the world are dominated, that world of which St. John speaks when he declares: "The friendship of the world is enmity against God, that world which lieth in the arms of the wicked one, that world which is ruled by the Prince of Darkness, that is, the Devil." Never has the world showed itself more dominating, more menacing than it does today, and to stand fast true to the Faith and face it in all its power requires really heroic courage. How imperiously it endeavours to bring all beneath its sway and impose its fashions and outlook upon all: "Why, if you are not in the fashion, you might as well be dead," how often you hear an expression like this used as a justification for capitulating to the fashion of the moment. But what says the Apostle? "Be not conformed to the fashion of this world, because the fashion of this world passes away," and again St. Paul exhorts us to be dead to the world but alive unto God. The whole atmosphere of the world is one of revolt against God: "For the spirit of this world is not subject to the Spirit of God, neither can be." Hence as long as we live we are in conflict.

And we are in conflict with the flesh, our own flesh, because if the spirit is willing the flesh is weak, and always ready to cry out for a little more ease, a little more comfort, a little more pleasure, a little less renunciation. Now the world is an external foe, and, powerful though it be, is less to be feared than an enemy within the gate.

There are moments of utter exhaustion and weakness, so that when the time for rising comes we feel that if we move we must die, but with a desperate effort we do get up, and find that after all we do not die quite so easily as we imagined. At times like these when Nature cries out for ease, we must keep before our mind the way our brave little Leader acted. See her, with her head spinning round with a terrible vertigo, going to office in choir because one foot could follow the other, or at the end of her life, when her sufferings had increased so much that it

34

was a hard struggle to mount the stairs, and when finally she reached her cell she was so exhausted that it took an hour to undress. And we must note, too, how bravely she hid all her sufferings behind a smiling countenance, so that very few had any idea of the torment she was enduring. That was her way of giving little sacrifices to Jesus.

Finally, there is the Devil, who, when he has used the first two methods of attack in vain, flings himself upon the soul in all his fury in one tremendous assault, just when the soul is most exhausted after combat with the other two.

So it was in the last year of the life of the Virgin of Lisieux. Thick darkness enwrapped her soul, from out of which voices mocked at her faith, assuring her that this darkness should be succeeded by a night yet darker, a night of utter nothingness, but as she says, never in all her life had she made so many acts of faith as then, she met all the assaults of the evil one with this affirmation of faith, declaring her readiness to give her blood for it.

We have all at some time experienced these moments of conflict with the Powers of Darkness, a combat compared with which the struggles against the world and the flesh seem as almost nothing. But yet in the midst of the most intense combat the deep interior peace of the soul is not disturbed, because we can only lose that peace if we give admittance to the enemy.

Life, then, is one long unceasing combat, in which the modes of attack and the forces of the enemy are constantly changing, sometimes the assault comes from one direction, sometimes from another, sometimes from all three combined, but if we follow the example and teaching of our holy little Mistress we shall always be victorious.

There are moments, of course, when the Devil penetrates

our defences, but we must counter-attack, and with the grace of God to sustain us we shall regain the ground which has been lost. We must always be watchful and vigilant, but especially at moments of comparative tranquillity, for we may be sure the enemy of all good is preparing some new form of attack. I remember one afternoon on the battle-front for a while the rush of shells had ceased, and I remarked to a soldier, "It is so quiet you could hardly believe there was a war on." "Far too quiet for my liking," was his reply, and hardly were the words spoken before shells were crashing all around us. So it is in spiritual warfare, quiet moments are the most dangerous, hence never for a second must we be off our guard.

Our little Saint was so much attracted to St. Jeanne d'Arc because she was a soldier, and she makes the words of the Maid of Orleans her own: "We must *fight* in order that God may give us the victory," indeed, very often the words she puts into the mouth of her heroine are the expression of her own feelings. Listen to this:

"For You, my God, my father I forsake.
My parents dear, my beloved church tower,
For You I go forth to fight in the war.
I hear the battle-shout of those in combat
I want the cross, I love the sacrifice.
How sweet to suffer for Your Love, my Lord Jesus, my beloved, for You I am ready to die."

It might be the battle-song of St. Thérèse as she goes to Carmel.

She well understood the nature of the war in which she was engaged, and in her prayer for courage says: "Lord God of Armies, in Your Gospel you have said, *'I have not come to bring peace, but a sword'*; I burn with longing to battle for Your glory,

I beg You to increase my courage, then with Holy King David I shall cry, You, O Lord, have taught my hands to war . . . Jesus, I will fight for Your love till the evening of my life. As You never sought repose upon earth, I shall follow Your example."

She turns to St. Sebastian: "O Glorious Soldier of Christ, give me your aid. I must redden with my blood the arena of combat. Mighty warrior, be my protector, sustain me with your victorious arms, then I shall not fear all the might of the enemy. With your aid I shall fight on till the evening of my life."

One day in the July before her death one of her sisters said to her: "You may well rejoice, for you will soon be freed from the sufferings of this life."

"I rejoice at that? Oh, no!" she replied, and then added, with a wan smile: "I who am such a valiant soldier!" And speaking to her favourite Blessed Theophane Venard, she exclaims:

> "Soldier of Christ, ah! give me your arms,
> For sinners would I fight down here,
> Suffer, give my blood, my tears;
> Protect me, sustain my arms.
> For them I could never cease to war
> Till I take by assault the Kingdom of the Lord,
> For the Lord has come to earth
> Not to bring peace, but fire and sword."

She realized very well that the fight against one's self and one's natural weaknesses was infinitely more important than extreme physical penances, which are self-chosen.

She refers to a passage which impressed her much in the life of Blessed Henry Suso. He had used the most frightful physical penances, and half ruined his health by so doing, when an angel appeared to him and said: "You are no longer to fight as a simple soldier but as a knight," and then made him realize the superiority of spiritual mortifications as compared with physical. "Very well," she went on, "God does not wish me to fight as a simple soldier. He has armed me as a knight, and I have engaged in war against myself in the spiritual sphere by secret sacrifices. I have found humility and peace in this hidden warfare, where Nature finds nothing for herself."

The Devil very often tries to distract the soul from this essential warfare by suggesting some extraordinary penances which will produce exactly the result he desires.

No, if we are to be faithful to the teaching of our beloved Mistress we shall seek no extraordinary mortifications, but instead work without ceasing to overcome ourselves, to master our weaknesses, to restrain our tongue, to be silent when provoked, go on when we feel tired and worn out, bear with a smile the crosses and the little irritations which must be ours as long as we live. Perhaps the day has been long, the work heavy, and just as we feel it is over at last someone comes along to ask us to give a hand, as we have not had much to do! To give the help asked, and give it with a smile, no matter how tired nature may be inclined to complain, this is what we have to do.

We must endure hardship as good soldiers of Christ, for war involves hardship; we must not expect rest but labour, not quiet but conflict. One day the war will be over, one day all the warrior hosts of light will stream in triumph through the gates of the city of God. The dark night of earth is past, the day of eternal light and eternal peace has come at last, a day which shall never end. If we bear our part bravely on the battlefield of time, we shall rejoice in the everlasting peace of Heaven: *"We shall be there!"*

CHAPTER IV
THE APOSTOLATE OF SACRIFICE AND SUFFERING

ACRIFICE and suffering, although intimately related, are two different things. Sacrifice is something freely and willingly offered to God, while suffering is something endured.

Sacrifice inevitably implies suffering, but suffering does not necessarily imply sacrifice. Of the Supreme Sacrifice of Calvary offered by the Eternal Son to the Eternal Father it is written: "He was sacrificed because He willed it," and Our Saviour Himself declared: "I lay down my life that I may take it again. No one taketh it away from me, but I lay it down of myself;" all of which makes clear the voluntary nature of sacrifice.

But this Supreme Sacrifice involved a suffering proportioned to the greatness of the sacrifice, for in the Garden of the Agony the Saviour cried out as He beheld the full extent of the torment: "Father, if it be possible let this chalice pass from me," this chalice which, as St. Thérèse remarks, before He had so eagerly desired to drink, and in the impenetrable darkness of Calvary that suffering wrung from the heart of the Saviour the exceedingly bitter cry: "My God, my God, why hast Thou forsaken me?"

And we, too, in the small sacrifices which we make, offer them freely to Jesus, and we, like Him, must in our degree experience the pain which necessarily accompanies sacrifice; for the freedom with which we make the sacrifice takes nothing from the pain experienced in offering it. St. Paul urges us to offer our bodies as a living sacrifice, holy and acceptable to God, which is our reasonable service.

A sacrifice, then, which will always be in progress until the day of our death: "For Thy sake are we being sacrificed all the day long." "True love nourishes itself upon Sacrifice, and the more a soul denies herself natural satisfactions the stronger and more disinterested becomes her affection." These words of our saintly Mistress put in their right relationship the thoughts always inseparable in her mind: love and sacrifice. The strength of our love is measured by what we are ready to sacrifice for the Beloved; in another place she says: "There is but one thing to do down here: to throw Jesus the flowers of little sacrifices and win Him by caresses, this is what I have done, and that is why I shall be so well received." "Little sacrifices," our holy Patroness calls them, but they may appear very big to us, for very often these apparently small sacrifices cost more than the greater one, just as the scratch of a pain may cause more pain than a deep wound.

St. Thérèse uses the words suffering and sacrifice as interchangeable. Why? Because she always transformed all her sufferings into sacrifices. She lovingly, willingly, eagerly embraced each suffering as it befell her and offered it as a sacrifice to Jesus, for by this act of her will she made the suffering her own just as if by a deliberate act she had chosen it herself.

Suffering is inevitable for us all in this world, for we are all soldiers engaged in warfare, and warfare necessarily involves sacrifice and suffering.

Now suffer we must whether we will it or not; everything

depends on how we endure it. We can rebel against the inevitable and cry out that God is cruel and unjust to let us suffer so, what have we done that we should endure all this anguish? But cry out as we may, the suffering must be undergone all the same, and our resistance rather increases than diminishes our pain.

Again we can submit, because we know resistance is vain, we do not enquire why the suffering has befallen us, perhaps we are too much crushed to do so; in any case, we submit, feeling that "the ways of the Lord are past finding out." That is resignation. If we could find a way of escape from the suffering, very gladly would we do so, but realizing that this is impossible we resign ourselves to bearing it as best we may. But there is a third way: we can embrace the suffering, readily, gladly, willingly offering it to Jesus with loving affection, glad to be accounted worthy to suffer for His sake. Then our suffering becomes a sacrifice well-pleasing in His sight. That is the way our holy little Mistress would have us walk, that is how she would have us behave under suffering: she has shown to us the way because she changed all her sufferings into sacrifices by the loving eagerness with which she embraced them.

"Suffering," she writes, "held out its arms to me from my very entrance into Carmel, and I have embraced it lovingly . . . the more crosses I encountered the more my attraction to suffering increased." Sacrifice involves choice and as we study the doctrine of our Saint a question arises concerning her donation of her will to God, for if she has given up her will entirely into His hands, where is the freedom which would seem to be necessary to her if her sufferings are really to be sacrifices? First of all, we must have a right idea of what freedom really is. Freedom, says St. Thomas, is when the will

41

remains intrinsically indifferent to one thing or another.

This freedom for the Blessed consists in the choice of this or that, but always in the order of good.

This freedom for the damned consists in the choice of this or that, but always in the order of evil.

This freedom for us upon earth consists in our choice of this or that, either good or evil. Our freedom, then, consists in this, that we can choose Heaven or Hell, life or death, salvation or damnation; a terrible freedom, one which may well make us afraid.

Now St. Thérèse did deliberately and willingly on the day of her first Communion make the sacrifice of this freedom as regards liberty to choose evil, for she says: "Thérèse had disappeared like a drop of water in the ocean, Jesus alone remained; He was the master, the king! Had not Thérèse asked Him to take away her freedom. *That freedom which made her afraid.* She felt herself to be so frail, so feeble, that she would be for ever united with the Divine strength."

Why did that freedom make her afraid? Because of the possibility it afforded of offending her Divine Lover, and she desired to be freed from this freedom.

"Often," she writes, "I repeated that passage of the *Imitation of Christ:* 'O Jesus, ineffable sweetness, change for me into bitterness all the consolation of earth.' Those words rose to my lips without effort, I uttered them like a child who repeats without very well understanding words inspired by some dear friend." When near death, she gave an explanation of the sense in which she used these words: "I did not pray to be deprived of divine consolation, but only of those joys and illusions which so often turn aside the soul from God," in which she echoes the thought of the Royal Psalmist: "Turn away mine eyes lest they behold vanity."

In her act of oblation she is still more explicit as to the liberty which she surrenders to God: "I beseech You to take from me the freedom by which I can displease You." It was that liberty by which she could be fascinated and allured by the things of time, by which she might offend her Divine Lover, which she asked Him to take from her: "How can a heart given over to human affection be intimately united to God? I feel it is impossible. I have seen souls seduced by that false light cast themselves into it like poor butterflies and burn their wings, afterwards to return wounded to Jesus, the divine fire which burns without consuming."

Here below, then, our freedom is such that on the one hand it has a certain resemblance to the blessed in Heaven, and on the other to that of the damned in Hell. From this latter freedom she would be freed, and surely all the disciples of our little Mistress will make her desire their own; they would be delivered from that freedom which may well make them afraid, seeing it can involve the loss of the soul.

But our little Mistress went further and made the complete surrender of her will to choose even in the order of good.

Speaking of an incident of her childhood she writes: "One day Léonie, no doubt feeling herself too grown up to play with dolls, finding us both together (herself and Celine) brought a basket filled with dolls' frocks and other trifles, on top of which she had placed her doll, saying: 'Here, darlings, choose as you like.' Celine looked into it and took a woollen ball. After reflecting for a moment I put out my hand saying, '*I choose all,*' and without more ado carried off both doll and basket. . . . That incident of my childhood sums up the whole of my life. Later on when the way of perfection was opened out before me . . . I realized that there are numerous degrees of sanctity, and that each soul is free to respond to the advances of Our Lord and to do little or much for His Love; in a word, to *choose* between the sacrifices which He demands. Then, as in the days of my childhood, I cried 'My God, *I choose all!* I will not be a saint by halves. I am not afraid to suffer for You. I fear only one thing, that is to retain my own will: *take it, for I choose all that You will.'"*

The choice she made was to put all her own freedom into God's freedom, so that henceforth His choice and hers should be one and the same. By this one act she offered the living sacrifice of her freedom for the rest of her life.

Only a few days before her death Mother Agnes (her Sister Pauline) said to her: "Would you rather die than live?" "O my little mother," she replied, "I repeat again that I do not prefer one to the other. What pleases God best, and He chooses for me, this is the thing which pleases me most." Earlier in the year she said: "I do not wish to die rather than to live. I leave it to God to *choose* for me. What He does pleases me."

She has not lost her freedom by this immolation, rather she has gained it, since now she has the freedom of God, and her will is so made one with His that while the two wills remain distinct they act as one.

Did she fully realize all the tremendous consequences involved in this heroic act? Yes, for she writes later on: "When the way of perfection was opened out before me I realized that to become a saint one must *suffer much, seek always that which is the most perfect, and forget oneself.*"

She was under no illusion, she must *suffer much,* and that suffering she embraced lovingly, joyously, for she herself says: "I have found happiness and joy only in suffering." Again, "Long since *has suffering* become my heaven here below, and I find it hard to conceive how it will be possible to become acclimatized in a country where joy reigns supreme without any admixture of sorrow." And again, "For one trial borne with joy we shall love God the more for all eternity." And in her act of immolation, "I thank You, O God, for all the graces You have bestowed upon me in particular for having made me pass through the crucible of suffering."

Then when the great darkness descended upon her which enclosed all the last year of her life she exclaimed: "Notwithstanding this trial which deprived me of *all feeling of joy*, I can say, 'You have given me, O Lord, delight in Your doings,' for is there a greater joy than to suffer for love?"

"I received no consolation from heaven or earth, and yet in the midst of the waters of tribulation *I was the happiest of beings*," surely she echoes the thought of St. Paul, "as sorrowing yet always rejoicing."

This amazing paradox of the supernatural life, joy in the midst of sufferings, smiles in the midst of tears, must be experienced in order fully to be understood.

For the joy in suffering of St. Thérèse was not a sensible joy but a *joy unfelt*, for as she said, "If you desire *to feel* joy in order to have an attraction for suffering, then it is consolation which you seek, for pain disappears when we love something."

One day during the August preceding her death she said: "I was thinking of those words of St. Ignatius of Antioch. 'I, too, by suffering must be ground down so as to become the fine wheat of God.'" This unfelt joy in the midst of suffering is the effect of love which rejoices not in suffering itself but in suffering for the loved.

Now, we may ask, must all the disciples of St. Thérèse follow her in this tremendous immolation of the will, even in the order of good? No, it is not a question of must, but of may. All are not compelled to make this immolation, but all may do so, for as she herself perceived, there is a choice amongst good, and each soul is free to give little or much in response to the invitation of the Saviour.

But the soul who wishes to be truly generous will answer with St. Thérèse: "I choose all . . . take my will, I give it you." She will say: "Jesus, do with me what You please, and I shall be pleased with what You do." She does not know what the future holds, but she has made the full surrender of everything to the Divine Lover, she has chosen all that He wills for her. Does she realize what is involved in it? Perhaps no more than did the two apostles who in reply to the question of the Saviour: "Can you drink of the chalice of which I shall drink, and be baptized with the baptism wherewith I shall be baptized?" replied so very confidently, "Yes, we can."

But St. Thérèse saw that this choice also involved always doing that which was most perfect, that which was most pleasing to the heart of God. Of two ways of offering something to Jesus, the one which allows least to nature is the one which will please Him the most. This is how we must act in all the varied circumstances of life. Always going against nature, and never allowing it the least indulgence. How heroically our little Mistress fulfilled this part of her choice.

Finally, to forget oneself was likewise part of her: "I choose all."

"O Jesus, grant that none may trouble themselves about me, that I may be forgotten, trodden underfoot like a little grain of sand. . . . I no longer wish for anything but to be forgotten. . . . Neither contempt nor injuries do I seek. These would be too glorious for the 'grain of sand,' because to despise a grain of sand one must see it and think about it." Again, "What happiness to be so completely hidden that no one thinks about you—to be unknown even to those who live with you."

When quite a child she realized that "true glory which

endures forever does not consist in the performance of great works, but rather in hiding ourselves from the eyes of others and even from oneself." To forget oneself entirely is by no means easy to nature, but it is easy to grace, for the more grace enlightens the soul the better she perceives her own nothingness. It is so essential for us to realize that we are nothing and can do nothing, that we are absolutely dependent upon God for everything we have and are both naturally and supernaturally!

"Through much tribulation we must enter the Kingdom of Heaven," this means sacrifice and suffering.

And each day as it comes brings with it another day in which the living sacrifice is being offered to God, each day brings its own special cross and its own special suffering, and each day will go on bringing its quota till the last day of all.

And these little sacrifices, what are they? Someone makes a very unpleasant remark very pointedly directed at myself. Well, I am silent, and make as if I had not heard it; and take the opportunity of speaking kindly to the one who has wounded me when the opportunity offers, and take good care to forget immediately the words which have hurt me. I go out of my way to be kind to one who is naturally awkward and left-handed, one whom others avoid. St. Thérèse won her way by her sweet smile, and a smile and a kind word go far, even with those who are naturally difficult to get on with.

To smile and hide our sufferings from others, to go on when we feel we cannot, when if we take another step we must drop, this is the way in which to turn our sufferings into sacrifices. Often this terrible sense of exhaustion is far harder to bear than actual pain, and we need the Divine Strength itself to enable us to do so. But we must never give in, no matter how we feel, for our little Mistress says we ought to go to the

47

very limit of our strength.

During the course of each day there are always occasions, small it is true, but none the less real occasions for sacrifice. Someone else has taken our turn, which delays us, just when we are almost at the end of our task, or, when for a moment we have been called aside to attend to something else, someone borrows some instrument we were using, of course without telling us they are taking it. Then, when we come back, there is the search for the missing instrument, finally we trace it, and the one who has carried it off hands it back without a word of explanation. These things are trifles in themselves, but they mount up during the day, and if we can thank Jesus for sending them and have a smile all the time we may feel we are really following in the footsteps of our holy Mistress and putting into practice the things which she has taught us.

CHAPTER V
THE APOSTOLATE OF SOULS

T was love alone which inspired our beloved Patroness with that intense zeal for souls which characterized her whole life: just as it was love alone which inspired her with that passion for sacrifice and suffering which was likewise so characteristic of her. It was her love of God and her desire that others should love Him with a fervour like her own which made her such an ardent apostle. For it was in order that these souls should love Him eternally that she desired their salvation rather than for their own happiness. This she has expressed very clearly:

"My God, I want to labour for Your Love alone, with the single end of giving You pleasure, of consoling Your Sacred Heart and of saving souls *who shall love You eternally.*"

Not long before her death when speaking of her future apostolate she said: "I feel that now my mission is about to begin, my mission of making others love God as I have loved Him," and in a letter to one of her missionaries: "What draws me towards the Eternal Fatherland is the call of the Lord, the hope of loving Him at last as I have so ardently desired, and the thought that I shall be able to make Him loved by a multitude of souls who shall love Him eternally."

Her attraction to sacrifice and suffering sprang from her desire to suffer and sacrifice herself for her love. "In my childhood on awakening in the morning, I used to think over the happenings, sad or joyful, which I might meet during the day; and if I foresaw only trying events, I rose dispirited. Now it is quite the contrary; thinking of the difficulties or sufferings which await me, I rise all the more joyously and full of courage the more I foresee opportunities of proving my *love to Jesus.*"

Again she sings:

"Neath suffering's bitter winepress
I will prove my love to Thee.
To immolate myself each day
My chosen joy shall be."

Our little Mistress relates how first this passion to save souls was begotten in her heart. "One Sunday as I closed my book at the end of Mass, a photograph of Our Saviour crucified slipped sideways showing one of His hands pierced and bloodstained. I experienced a new inexpressible sensation. My heart was filled with grief at seeing the Precious Blood fall to the earth without a soul to gather it. I resolved to remain continually in spirit at the foot of the Cross, receiving the Divine Blood and scattering it upon souls.

"From that day the cry of Jesus dying 'I thirst' resounded at each instant in my heart, kindling in it a zeal unknown before. I would give my Beloved to drink; I felt myself devoured with thirst for souls, and I desired at any price to snatch them from the eternal flames." The conversion of an anarchist at the very moment of execution gave her a sign that Jesus was pleased with her apostolate, and this redoubled her zeal. "After that unique grace," she continues, "my desire to save souls increased each day. I seemed to hear Jesus say to me as He did to the Good Samaritan 'Give me to drink.' It was a veritable exchange of love; I poured out the blood of Jesus upon souls, and to quench His thirst I offered to Jesus these same souls bedewed with the crimson of Calvary. But the more I gave Him to drink the greater became the thirst of my own poor soul, and this indeed was my most precious reward."

At her entry into Carmel she replied to the question as to why she had come with the words: "To save souls and pray for priests." What was it that attracted her to Heaven? Her reply to a sister who was speaking to her of the happiness of Heaven gives the answer:

"It is not that which attracts me."

"What is it, then?"

"It is love! To love and to be loved, and return to earth *to win love for our Love.*"

Again, "Like the Prophets and Doctors I would be a light unto souls. I would traverse the whole world to preach Your Name, O my Beloved, and raise upon heathen lands the glorious standard of the Cross. One mission alone would not satisfy my longings. I would spread the Gospel in every quarter of the globe, even to the farthest isles. I would be a missionary not for a few years only, but, were it possible, from creation's dawn until the end of the world."

On another occasion she exclaims: "Souls, Lord, we must have souls. Above all, souls of apostles and martyrs, that through them we may inflame the multitudes of poor sinners with love for You." And to one of her missionaries she writes: "Confidently I count on not being inactive in Heaven, my desire is to continue to work for souls; I have asked this of God, and I am certain that He has heard me ... the only thing I desire is to make God to be loved. I avow that if I could no longer work for this in Heaven, I should prefer exile to Fatherland."

Again, "I shall spend my Heaven in doing good upon earth. ... No, there will be no rest for me until the end of the world. But when the angel shall declare that 'Time shall be no more,' then I shall take my rest, then I shall be able to rejoice because the number of the elect will be complete."

Even on the very day of her death the heart of our little Mistress was still set on her apostolate for souls, turning to Mother Agnes she said: "Never would I have believed it possible to suffer so much! Never! Never! I can only explain it by the ardent desires I have had to save souls."

And the desires of our heavenly Mistress have been fulfilled to the full, her apostolate has reached to every land, over the whole earth she is gathering together a multitude of souls who are striving to follow in her steps and love God as she has loved Him. She vanquishes all opposition, brings hope to the hopeless, and shows them that however great their sin there is salvation for them through the Blood of Christ. And we are all called to take our part with her in this apostolate for souls:

"Let us work together to save souls; we have only the single day of this life in which to do so, and give to the Lord this proof of our love." These words of our saintly Mistress written to one of her missionaries the year before her death, may well apply to us.

Have not the disciples of St. Thérèse pledged themselves to imitate the apostolic spirit of St. Thérèse of the Child Jesus, by praying for vocations and the sanctification of priests, religious and missionaries, and aiding them in their ministry?

The Holy Father has again and again called upon the Faithful to take their part in this apostolate in union with the Hierarchy. How shall we bear our part in this apostolate? How shall we become apostles of souls? By prayer and hidden sacrifice. Prayer is the most potent weapon we can wield, because it reaches everywhere, pierces every barrier, triumphs over every obstacle, and as Pius XI has so often pointed out, the apostolate of prayer is within the reach of all, for there is not a soul in the whole world who cannot pray. Not all can be preachers of the Gospel, not all can be evangelists, not all can be missionaries, but all can pray, and in this way have part in the great apostolate.

First of all they can aid the priests of their own parish by their prayers, and by upholding them in their work. Even if they find defects in them, want of zeal and earnestness, they can help to remedy these defects by prayer. How much evil would be averted if, instead of talking about the defects or failings of a priest, his people set to work to pray for him. But prayer must not be limited to our own little circle, like our holy Mistress we must reach out and embrace the world, pray for all who labour for souls at home or abroad, and wherever priests and missionaries labour our prayers must accompany them. "My whole strength lies in prayer and sacrifice, these are my invincible arms, far better than words can they move hearts. I know it by experience," so says the Saint of Lisieux.

However poor and feeble we are, we can be apostles; listen to this example which our beloved little saint gives us: "Sister Mary of the Eucharist wanted to light the candles for a procession; she had no matches, but seeing a little lamp burning before the relics she approached it, to find only a feeble glimmer remaining on the burnt wick. Nevertheless she succeeded in lighting her candle, and by means of that candle all those of the community. Then I said to myself: 'Who can glory in His works?' See how this little flame, almost extinguished as it was, has been able to produce all these lights, which in turn can light an infinite number of others and finally embrace the whole world. And yet it is always this humble little lamp which remains as the first cause of all this fire."

It is the same in the communion of saints. One very little spark can beget great lights in the Church like the doctors and martyrs. Often without our being aware of it the graces and lights which we receive are due to some hidden soul because God wills that the saints communicate His grace from one to another by prayer, in order that in heaven they may love each other with a greater love, a love exceeding that of any family, even the most ideal upon earth. How many times I have thought that perhaps all the graces I have received are due to the prayers of some little soul who has obtained them for me from God, and whom I shall never know till I get to Heaven.

Surely here is encouragement and consolation for us in those moments when we realize how very weak and miserable we are, and are inclined to say: "Of what avail can my prayers be with God." It was just that little dying light which gave light to all those candles, hence how can I know what my poor little prayers and feeble sacrifices may not obtain from the loving Heart of God. The communion of saints, how immensely consoling it is, this communion of saints on earth, in heaven, in purgatory! For we are all called to be saints, since the will of God is our sanctification and the Divine Lover Himself calls us to be perfect as our heavenly Father is perfect. How can we become perfect? Only by love. Love will bring us to perfection. Love will enable us to triumph over our weakness and become strong with all the strength of God, for nothing is impossible to Love.

As the fire of love increases within us our prayers and sacrifices will increase too, our zeal for the salvation of souls will become intensified; we shall want to draw all the souls we can to love God, and our desire to save them will be the same as that which inspired our holy Mistress: that God may have more souls to love Him eternally; thus shall we be her true disciples, animated by her spirit and treading in her footsteps.

Our life may be passed in the most humble and hidden round of daily duty, we may be as little observed as the very tiny grain of sand which is trodden underfoot in the streets, yet we are apostles of souls, for as our little Saint says: "Jesus desires that the salvation of souls shall be achieved by our sacrifices and our love. Let us offer our sufferings to Jesus to save them."

CHAPTER VI
THE DAY WITH ST. THÉRÈSE

THE Catholic religion is of value to the extent that it is translated into terms of life, and applied to every action and duty of our state day by day. Our whole life must be supernaturalized, each act performed in order to give pleasure to the heart of Jesus. Our beloved Patroness realized this to the full, nothing was too great and nothing too small to give to her Divine Lover. We who are the disciples of St. Thérèse must found our life upon her example and teaching, so that her doctrine becomes a part of ourselves and enters into every department of our life. How shall we spend the day in company with our beloved Mistress?

We must have a fixed hour for rising, so fixed as to allow sufficient time for prayer and preparation to meet the demands of the day before us. A fixed hour at which we rise regardless of what we feel like and the claims of tired nature which asks for a little more sleep. Immediately the hour has struck we must be up, out and on our knees. Jesus is calling, so we must respond. We give our tiredness and exhaustion as a morning gift to Him.

Remember prayer, as our holy Patroness understood it, is not reading something out of a book, but a loving, confiding, affectionate conversation with Jesus.

First of all we thank Jesus for having protected us from harm during the night and brought us to the beginning of another day in which we may love and serve Him. Then we glance forward to the day which is just beginning, what we shall have to do, what difficulties we must encounter, what temptations we must face during the hours that must run between morn and eve. We are only concerned with *this* day to which we have come, not with tomorrow, still less with the days, weeks, months, and years which may be before us. No, we have only to face today, for tomorrow when it comes will be today.

> "Keep Thou my feet, I do not ask to see
> The distant scene, one step enough for me."

How like these words of Cardinal Newman to those of St. Thérèse:

> "Do I pray for tomorrow? No, that I cannot do.
> Keep my heart pure, cover me with Thy wings
> Just for today."

We turn to our Jesus and offer Him everything that we shall think, do, say and suffer during the day, every beating of our heart, every breath, all for His Glory and the salvation of souls. We want to exist solely to please Him, and the stronger our love the stronger this desire will be. Knowing we can do nothing of ourselves we ask Jesus to be our strength and stay during the day, above all that He keep us pure, chaste and modest in all our thoughts, words, looks and actions. The most precious treasure we possess is chastity, more precious than aught else in the world, and because so precious it is the treasure most easily injured. So we must be ever on our guard that no word, glance or thought may tarnish it in the slightest degree.

We live in the midst of a world which has forgotten what chastity is, hence we need all the more vigilance in guarding ourselves from the soul-destroying atmosphere in which we have to live.

Then we ask our Jesus to make us sweet, gracious and gentle in our dealings with those with whom we have to do, no matter whether they are so to us or not. It is not difficult to be gracious and gentle with those who are so, but it costs a great deal to be so with those who are not.

Again we have to be humble, calm and patient under the trials and difficulties which may befall us and remember that, however heavy they be, God from all eternity saw we should have to face them today, at the very moment and in the very manner in which they befall us. If we bear them humbly and patiently, then we are really doing something for Jesus and the salvation of souls.

Listen to this; it comes from one leading a hard strenuous life on a farm out in the Colonies. It was Christmas Eve, and he had the task of taking the stock to town to sell. Just on the outskirts of the town the lorry broke down and nothing he could do succeeded in moving it. The only thing to do was to tramp to and round the city and dispose of it on foot. Then a long weary walk of four and half miles back, thinking all the while of how he was to get the heavy load of dressed poultry back to town and delivered that night. Let him continue the story: "On arriving home I found my partner working hard, and eleven dressed already, then I got to work and we soon hurried up. At half-past eight all is ready, the load is heavy and a long way to go, I need help, but my partners are tired out and refuse to lend a hand. My thoughts for the moment were not too good for those of the household, but I try to find excuses for them, for these thoughts were merely natural, and so far Our Dear Lord had no opportunity to share my heavy burden. I start off with my big box on my head, but can only go three hundred yards, and with difficulty get it to the ground. It is too heavy for my head, so I raise it to my shoulder but can only manage fifty yards, then with both hands manage two hundred more, with eight or nine rests. While sitting saying my prayers, the Good Samaritan comes along in the shape of a black fellow who is a good friend of mine, so with a good heart I ask if he will help me, but he, too, is tired out, and says 'No!' Time is getting on, and there is the Midnight Mass. Can I hope to get all my business over in time, my black friend has gone, I make another effort for a short distance. I have enough patience left to thank Our Sweet Jesus for all the refusals of natural help, with the assurance that His strength is sufficient for me. With renewed courage I pick up my burden and put it on my head and carry it with ease for a mile and a half; for this time I am not alone, Jesus is with me to take the heaviest part of the load. A rest to recite my rosary, and soon after I am there delivering my orders. I finished at half-past eleven in good time for Mass." This is the way to face the trials of life, in the true spirit of our little Saint, whose courage rose higher as her sufferings increased.

Listen to our holy Mistress: "I want you to be like a valiant soldier who forgets his own wounds in thinking of the more grievous wounds of his brethren, esteeming his own as mere scratches."

Like her we must live solely for Jesus and ordering our day as did she, thus our every word, thought and action will give Him pleasure. Then we ask our sweet heavenly Mother Mary to obtain from the Heart of Jesus grace to meet our every need and keep this thought in mind: "She is my Mother just as if I was the only being in the whole universe, *my* Mother whom Jesus has given me with His dying breath upon Calvary." How wonderful that He should give His own Mother to me, to be mine, wholly mine. How can I ever love her enough and how ever thank Him enough for His wonderful gift.

Then I pray our sweet little Patroness "to come down" as she promised she would and stay beside me, so as to keep me in "her sure way," that way in which I can never be mistaken or go astray. I make the petition of that great lover of our little Saint, Benedict XV, my own:

"O Sweet little Thérèse of the Child Jesus, who in your brief earthly life became a mirror of angelic purity, strong love and generous *abandon* to God's will, now you rejoice in the reward of your virtue; cast a glance of compassion upon your child who confides in you. Make my afflictions your own, say a word for me to that Immaculate Virgin of whom you are the chosen flower, to that Queen of Heaven who smiled upon you in the morning of your life. Ask her as Mistress of the Heart of Jesus through her potent intercession to obtain for me the grace I so earnestly desire at this moment, and to accompany it with a benediction which may strengthen me in life, defend me in death and assure me a blessed eternity. Amen."

If by rising an hour earlier we can hear Mass and receive Jesus into our hearts we shall most certainly do so. How can we better begin the day than by being present at the Holy Sacrifice and giving a loving welcome to Jesus, who comes with all His Divine Strength to dwell within us.

If we can receive Jesus every day by the sacrifice of a little sleep, even if we do feel tired and exhausted, we shall rise eagerly and gladly and find often to our surprise that the tiredness vanishes once we have courageously resolved to conquer it.

How eagerly St. Thérèse desired to enjoy this most precious privilege, and how ardently she longed to see Daily Communion established at Carmel, and how great her consolation when, during the terrible epidemic of influenza which carried off so many of the sisters, she was allowed to receive Jesus every day.

I must try and value this great gift as she did. Who comes? Jesus Christ, God and man. God in all His Almightiness, in all His immensity, He who *is* Infinite Love, He who by a single word created the universe out of nought, sustains it in being, and who by a single word could annihilate it. Jesus comes in all the Power of His Divinity, in all the weakness of His Humanity, this Jesus who assumed our nature so as to agonize, suffer and die in it out of pure love for us, this Jesus comes, and comes to me. May I love Him, love Him, love Him, love Him and never do aught to wound and grieve Him again. To whom does He come? To a poor creature whom He has created out of nothing, absolutely dependent upon Him for existence from moment to moment. To one who has wounded and offended Him again and again, and yet in spite of all He comes, full of love for the most worthless and miserable of His creatures.

Why does He come? Love alone brings Him, because in spite of all my worthlessness He loves me, loves me as if I was the only soul existing in all His vast creation. He comes to transform me into Himself, for love fashions the one loved to its own likeness.

What can I say to this miracle of Love? Jesus, my own sweet adorable Jesus, come! I love You, I love You and wish to exist for You alone, I want each breath I draw to be all for You. Jesus, my own adorable Lover, the Lover of all my life, come to my heart.

I come away from the altar rails with strength renewed, strong not in my own strength but in His, assured that He is within me, and that so I can face whatever the day brings because He Himself will triumph in me: "I live, yet not I, Christ lives in me."

But if owing to our circumstances it is impossible to receive Jesus sacramentally each day, we may be able to spend a few moments before the Tabernacle and make an act of Spiritual Communion, or if that, too, is impossible, make the act before we leave the house. Let us speak to Jesus just as we feel inspired at the moment, in some such terms as these:

"My sweetest Jesus, come to my heart. I cannot have You sacramentally, but I will to receive You spiritually. Come, reign in my heart. I would love You more than all else in the whole of Your universe. Jesus, I want my heart to become a flame of love for You. Amen."

At meals always make the sign of the cross and invoke God's blessing on what you are about to partake before sitting down and never arise from table without giving thanks to Him for His Goodness.

The blessing that has the sanction of more than a thousand years is short and easy for all to remember: "Bless us, O Lord, and these Thy gifts which of Thy bounty we are about to partake. Amen."

And the thanksgiving is equally brief: "We give Thee thanks, O God, for all Thy benefits. Amen. May the souls of the faithful departed through the mercy of God rest in peace. Amen."

At each meal always make an act of penance, either by eating something you do not like, or going without something you do. Vary the mortification from time to time, but do not fail to do so. It is one of those hidden sacrifices which our little Mistress loved so well.

Never complain about food, take it just as it comes, overcooked, undercooked, lukewarm, hot or cold, it comes just as Jesus wants us to have it, and that is the only thing that matters. It is never worth while to make a fuss over food. If what you want is present, take it; if absent, go without it. Some people are never contented, the food is never to their liking, there is always something wrong. The disciples of St. Thérèse must take good care not to follow their example, but like their holy Mistress take what comes and give no sign of displeasure. Those sisters who observed our beloved Saint very closely in the Refectory, watched for years, without ever being able to discover what was her preference in food, as she took what was set before her without giving the slightest indication as to whether it was to her liking or not.

A great part of the day for most of us is occupied with the work in which we are engaged in order to gain the means of existence. It is quite true that work came at first as a punishment for sin: "In the sweat of thy brow shalt thou eat bread till thou return to the earth whence thou hadst been taken: for dust thou art and to dust thou shalt return." But redemption has sanctified work and made it a holy thing, for the Saviour Himself has toiled in the carpenter's shop at Nazareth. Yes, work comes to us as one of the most blessed gifts of God to man. Nothing brings so much good to soul and body as work well and honestly done with the sole intention of giving pleasure to Jesus and saving the souls for whom He has died.

The work may be hard, and still worse painfully uninteresting, the day long, but however long "at length the bell ringeth to evensong," and to go to rest tired out with honest work is the happiest ending to the day we can possibly have. Work occupies the mind and exercises the body; true, some work is painfully monotonous, such as is the lot of those condemned to labour in factories, where they are making the same thing year in and year out. Standing by the machine, for example, turning out the base of a candlestick, never seeing the completed article, for others are making the other parts and another hand will put them together. This is the reason that rebellion against work is nearly always found in the great industries, as they are called. The brass worker who gradually hammers out and builds up a candlestick, for example, has the pleasure of seeing his work gradually growing to completion till at length he can behold the finished article; a joy the industrial worker never knows. The most natural work of all for man is the cultivation of the land; for here man is in contact with nature and sees the works of God, the changes of seasons, the growth of the harvest, and is in surroundings which are helpful to contemplation. The same is true of those who work at the various arts, for they have the joy of seeing the realization of their conceptions.

But we must take the world as we find it and super-naturalize our work whether interesting or not, by doing it not for creatures, but for God. This work here and now, uninteresting as it is, this work Jesus has given me to do, and I am doing it to please Him. This thought changes the whole outlook, and makes that which before seemed an intolerable burden, to become light and even pleasant ; a joy instead of a penance. Not a joy in itself, but a joy in Him for whom it is done. I am not doing this to please a creature, who perhaps never can be pleased, however hard and however well I work, but I am working to please the Saviour Himself, who sees and understands all. Again and again during the day I must renew the offering of my work to Jesus, then I shall do it to the best that is in me, for I cannot give Him less than my very best. How many years my Jesus toiled hidden and unknown in the carpenter's shop at Nazareth, thirty years of life hidden and unknown to the three in which He manifested forth His glory, yet years not less fruitful for our redemption. Think, too, how Our Blessed Lady worked the day long just as we do. "The life at Nazareth," says our little Mistress, "was a life just like ours."

Idleness is the greatest curse that can befall us. We must never pass a moment in idleness. It opens the door to a thousand temptations, as the Devil knows full well. Idleness is the Devil's opportunity. A monk went to his Abbot one day and told him he was so overwhelmed with temptations that he knew not what to do. The Abbot sent him to help the cook in the monastery kitchen. A week later the Abbot met the monk and asked him about his temptations; the monk answered that he had been kept so busy that he had not had time for temptations.

Even if you do not have to labour for your living, never be idle. Spend eight hours a day on some useful work which will benefit others. For how many sins idleness is responsible! Look at our holy Patroness during her last illness; in spite of her suffering, she always had some work on hand so as never to be idle.

Most of us have to work whether we will it or not, and we should thank God every day for having disposed things thus, and saved us from a thousand temptations which would have befallen us had we been left with the whole day upon our hands:

"For Satan always finds work for idle hands to do." St. Paul speaks with no uncertain sound on the duty of work: "If a man will not work, neither shall he eat!"

Evening comes and we go to rest and sleep soundly because tired out with honest toil. We do not need a sleeping-draught like those unfortunate people who, having nothing to do, have spent the day killing time, and when night comes cannot sleep without some artificial aid. The best cure for sleeplessness is hard work, for then "rest after labour comes more sweet."

We enter the Church for a brief visit to Jesus, and sometimes are able to end the day by assisting at Benediction of the Blessed Sacrament. Anyhow, we spend some time in communion with Our Divine Lover, and then return home, where the family are all united after the day's work is done. How happy and joyous these evenings can be in families where natural and supernatural love reign supreme! Thank God there are many such, in which there reigns a sweet gladness which the world can never know.

But some of us perhaps are far away from home, and when we return to our solitary lodging a feeling of sadness and loneliness creeps over us. But we are not alone, Jesus is with us, within us, and He consoles and helps us with His blessed presence. Jesus knows our heart and He will satisfy it as He alone can.

Before I go to rest I kneel down and cast a rapid glance over the day that is past: Have I been pure, chaste and modest in all thoughts, words, looks and actions during the day?

Have I always been sweet, gracious and gentle in all my dealings with others, even if sometimes they have been the reverse?

Have I been as generous, as self-sacrificing and self-forgetting as a disciple of St. Thérèse ought to be?

Have I been calm and patient under the difficulties and trials which I have encountered during the day? Kept my temper no matter how much I may have been provoked? Have I done my work as perfectly as possible and offered it to Jesus?

For all in which I have failed I ask pardon of Jesus, for all in which I have triumphed I give thanks to Him, knowing full well that it is only His Presence in me which has enabled me to overcome. Then I ask Jesus to sprinkle His Blood upon myself and all dear to me, whether far or near, and upon all the world.

I beg our heavenly Mother to watch over me, and St. Thérèse to be with me, and obtain for me a quiet night's repose.

Finally, a prayer for all our loved ones who have gone before, then armed with the sign of the Holy Cross I lie down and take my rest.

This is the way to spend the day in company with our beloved Mistress; thus we shall be really worthy of her and so living we shall grow more and more like her, love of Jesus will increase, and we shall realize her prayer of loving Him as she has loved Him. Then when exile is over and the great day comes, when Jesus says: "Come," we shall be able to make our own His words to His Eternal Father, "I have finished the work Thou gavest me to do!"

CHAPTER VII
MASS WITH ST. THÉRÈSE

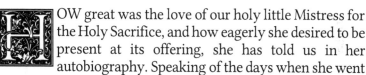

HOW great was the love of our holy little Mistress for the Holy Sacrifice, and how eagerly she desired to be present at its offering, she has told us in her autobiography. Speaking of the days when she went to Mass with her father she says: "Ah, the Feasts, what precious memories those simple words recall. . . . True, the great feasts came but seldom. Each week, however, brought one very dear to me—Sunday. What a glorious day! It was God's Feast and the day of rest. First of all, the whole family went to High Mass, and I remember before the sermon we had to leave our places, which were a good way from the pulpit, and find seats in the Nave." The place where St. Thérèse and her father used to sit for Mass in the Church of St. Pierre was a chapel on the epistle side of the choir from which there was a full view of the sanctuary, and it was in the Lady Chapel behind the choir that she used to hear Mass and go to Holy Communion on weekdays. St. Pierre is a glorious thirteenth-century building on the typical French plan, and its appearance is quite unchanged since the days when our little Saint had her place amongst its worshippers.

She herself ardently desired the priesthood, and was glad to die before the usual age for ordination so that she might not live regretting her deprivation of that sacred office. In that remarkable MS. which she wrote for her sister Marie she exclaims: "I would be a priest ... the vocation of the priesthood! With what love, my Jesus, would I bear You in my hands as my words brought You down from Heaven! With what love, would I give You to the Faithful!"

Let us then come and hear Mass in company with St. Thérèse. The prayers which follow are not for mere mechanical repetition, they are only suggestions of the way in which we may speak to God during the Holy Sacrifice. Use your own words, speak to Jesus as you feel inspired, for our Saint never used printed prayers, but spoke to her Divine Lover quite simply as would a child to its mother and father.

Having entered the church let us kneel down and make our prayer of preparation on lines something like these: Ask our little Mistress to help us to assist at the Holy Sacrifice with all the love and fervour possible:

"Thérèse of the Child Jesus, full of love and confidence I kneel before this altar, where Jesus is immolated for love of me. As I look at the little white Host uplifted I look upon Jesus sacrificed upon Calvary, the selfsame Victim, the selfsame Sacrifice. Dear little Mistress, may your ardent love, your virtue, your fervent devotion supply for my great insufficiency. I want to feel something of the fervour, something of the burning love which filled your heart when you, too, knelt before God's altar; I wish to love and adore Jesus in this Holy Sacrifice as you loved and adored Him."

While the priest is saying the *Confiteor* let us pray in some such words as these:

"O Thérèse of the Child Jesus, with what great love you burned towards God. and how truly the sacrifices and sufferings you endured so willingly for the salvation of souls gave proof of your love. And I, poor sinner, how many times have I offended Him, how often grieved and wounded Him.

"O Thérèse, although I am so poor and miserable, pray for me, intercede for me with our most sweet adorable Jesus. Your innocence, purity and humility are so pleasing to the Heart of God that I trust you will obtain for me a change of heart and a cure for my pride. Obtain also forgiveness for my faults, and may your efficacious protection make me partaker of your fidelity on earth and your glory in Heaven."

The prayers printed in italics are taken from the proper Mass of St. Thérèse.

INTROIT

"Come from Libanus, my spouse, come from Libanus; you have wounded my heart, my sister and my spouse, you have wounded my heart. Praise the Lord, ye children: praise the Name of the Lord. Glory be to the Father, and to the Son, and to the Holy Ghost: As it was in the beginning is now and ever shall be, world without end. Amen. Come from Libanus, etc."

"My most sweet Jesus, behold me here before You. I know full well I am not worthy to come into Your presence, but I know that your all-merciful love is infinite. I do want to please You and have You not said that whosoever comes to You, You will in no wise cast out. My sins and my manifold weaknesses discourage me, but I come in company with your holy virgin Thérèse, who in her innocence and virtue inspires me with immense confidence in Your goodness. I shall strive like her to keep close to You, and I unite my prayers and praise with hers, that so they may be more acceptable in Your sight."

At the KYRIE say something like this:

"O sweet and most adorable Jesus, have mercy upon me after Your great goodness, and according to the multitude of Your mercies do away with my offences. If You will regard what is done amiss how shall I dare to appear before You? O

Most Merciful Jesus, hear me through the intercession of Your beloved child Thérèse who desired to continue from Heaven her apostolate for souls and to send down upon us a rain of roses."

At the GLORIA:
"Glory be to God in the highest, and on earth peace to men of good will., O Jesus, my most adorable Saviour, You only are great, omnipotent, all-knowing, and all-merciful, have mercy on me and receive my prayer. Accept my adoring homage, and my loving service. I offer it in union with the love and adoration which Your holy Thérèse offered You when she was here upon earth.

"Vouchsafe to hearken to my prayer, and direct my heart in the way of peace, righteousness and mercy. Give me a great desire to please You in all I think, do, say and suffer, and grant me part in the gift of love which You bestowed upon our little Mistress Thérèse, that loving you fervently upon earth I may become one with You in Heaven."

At the COLLECT:
"O Lord, Who hast said, except ye become as little children ye shall not enter the Kingdom of Heaven, grant, we beseech Thee, thus to follow the holy virgin Thérèse in humility and simplicity of heart that we may obtain the reward of everlasting life. Who livest and reignest with God the Father and the Holy Ghost for ever and ever. Amen."

"O most pitiful and compassionate Jesus, as You have endowed Your humble virgin Thérèse with a heart full of pity and compassion for sinners, grant me, I beseech You, through her intercession, those graces of which I stand in need and which You see to be most necessary for me, that when life is over and I am liberated from the body of this death, I may be found worthy of Your divine embrace in the Heavenly

Country. Amen."

The EPISTLE:

"Thus saith the Lord, I shall make rivers of the nations like as a torrent which overflows its banks. You shall be nourished with milk, you shall be pressed to the breast, and caressed upon the knees. As one whom a mother caresses so will I comfort you, and you shall be consoled in Jerusalem. You shall see this and your heart shall rejoice and your bones shall flourish as the flowers of the field, and the Hand of the Lord shall shew them that He has loved you."

"O most adorable Jesus, make me humble and submissive to the truths contained in Your Divine Revelation, and all that Your Church teaches. Inspire me with that spirit of loving submission to the authority of Your Church which Your Thérèse manifested. May I serve You with something of her fervour and devotion, and may I be ever prompt to respond to the inspirations of Your Grace.

"My holy little Patroness, you were always so docile to the divine voice, and had such marvellous confidence in the Divine Goodness, hoping against hope you rested secure in the Divine Will; obtain for me the grace to imitate you in the faithful fulfilment of all the duties of my state both temporal and spiritual; that at each moment I may live in union with my adorable Jesus, and desire nothing save the perfect accomplishment of His Will."

At the GRADUAL:

"I bless You, Father of Heaven and earth, because You have hidden these things from the wise and prudent of this world and revealed them unto babes. O Lord, You have been my hope from my youth up.

"Alleluia, alleluia. You shall flourish like a rose tree planted by the rivers of waters. You shall give sweet perfume like

Lebanon. You shall flourish as the lily and give forth sweetness and increase in grace, You shall sing songs of praise and bless the Lord in all His works. Alleluia."

At the GOSPEL:

"Thérèse, obtain for me a great love for the Holy Gospels that like you I may find in them the hidden Manna, and everything of which my soul stands in need. Help me to put in practice the precepts of the Gospel, so that my whole life being lived in accordance therewith, I may find therein my joy and consolation."

The GOSPEL (Matt. xviii, 1-4):

"At that time the disciples came to Jesus and said to Him, 'Who is the greatest in the Kingdom of Heaven?' And Jesus calling to Himself a little child set him in the midst of them and said: 'Amen I say unto you, except you be converted and become as little children you shall not enter the Kingdom of Heaven. Whosoever therefore shall humble himself as this little child, he is the greatest in the Kingdom of Heaven.'"

At the CREDO:

"I believe, O Lord, all You have revealed and all Your Church proposes for my belief or shall hereafter propose. I believe with the most absolute submission of head and heart all that faith teaches me. I wish to believe with the same strong assurance with which Your beloved child Thérèse believed, whether in darkness or in light, and I wish like her to be ready to shed my blood for the Faith. I believe all Your Church teaches, and reject all that she rejects, and in this faith I will live and die.

"O Thérèse, my holy Mistress, obtain for me your *living* faith by which my whole life and conduct may be conformed to the *living* voice of Holy Church."

At the OFFERTORY:

"My soul doth magnify the Lord and my spirit hath rejoiced in God my Saviour, because He hath regarded the humility of His handmaiden. He that is mighty hath wrought great things in me."

"I offer, O Eternal Father, the sacrifice of Your well-beloved Son for Your Glory, for the Salvation of souls, for Your Church militant upon earth, and for the salvation of my own soul. I unite myself to You, my most sweet Saviour, offering myself as a living sacrifice for Your love alone.

"To supply for my weakness I offer to You, O Lord, all the loving adoration of My Immaculate Mother Mary, of St. Thérèse together with that of all the saints and angels in Heaven, and all the faithful on earth, and united with them I would sing my song of thanksgiving for all Your goodness and mercy and all the manifold gifts and benefits You have bestowed upon me."

At the LAVABO:

"O most adorable Saviour, cleanse my soul by the infusion of Your grace that I may serve You with a pure conscience in a chaste body. Amen."

At the SECRET:

"We beseech Thee, O Lord, that the holy prayers of Saint Thérèse Thy virgin may render our sacrifice acceptable in Thy sight; that so it may be received through the merits of her in whose honour it is offered. Through Our Lord Jesus Christ Thy Son who with Thee and the Holy Ghost liveth and reigneth for ever and ever. Amen."

At the PREFACE:

"How sweet and consoling this invitation to lift up my heart to You in heaven, my most adorable Jesus. With Mary Your Immaculate Mother, with Thérèse and all Your Angels and Saints I honour, reverence and adore Your Majesty, Your

Greatness and Your Magnificence.

"When shall I, freed from this prison of the flesh, unite my voice with the heavenly choirs who, immersed in the contemplation of Your Divinity, unceasingly do cry, Holy, Holy, Holy, Lord God Almighty, who was, who is, and who is to come. Hosanna in the highest. Blessed is He who comes in the Name of the Lord. Hosanna in the highest."

At the CANON:

"O Thérèse, most worthy spouse of Jesus, obtain for me through your intercession a most vivid impression of the sufferings of Jesus for my salvation; may His infinite merits be applied to my soul. Obtain for me the grace to love and follow Jesus faithfully until death, who for love of me perpetually immolates Himself upon the altar. O *Jesus*, scatter the blessings of Your Redemption over the whole Church, especially upon myself and all near and dear to me.

"Apply to all in abundant measure the fruit of this divine Sacrifice. Visit them with Your grace and keep them faithful to You in life and in death, like Your holy spouse Thérèse, who corresponded so faithfully to Your grace. O most sweet mother of God, intercede for us now and at the hour of our death."

At the CONSECRATION:

"O Jesus, true God and true man, verily present upon this altar I adore You, I praise You, I love You with all the strength of my heart and my soul. I behold You, Jesus, hidden beneath the roundness and whiteness of the host, the God who made all things of nought, the God who holds the world in being; the *Man* who has redeemed the world. I adore You, Jesus, truly present in all the splendour of Your Divinity and all the strength of Your Humanity.

"O sweet Immaculate Mother, you adored this Divine Redeemer at His birth, you served Him during His earthly life, consoled Him in His sorrows, stood beneath the Cross with your sword-pierced heart and saw Him die; offer to Him your adoration in this most Blessed Sacrament, and by the fervour of your loving praise supply for my incapacity.

"O Thérèse of the Child Jesus, you whose soul burnt with such a flame of ardent love towards Jesus in this most Holy Sacrament, help me to love Him as I ought, especially at this most wonderful moment when His sacrifice is before my eyes.

"My adorable and most loving Jesus, in the multitude of Your mercies and the fullness of Your grace I commend to you all those who have preceded me into eternity, especially the soul of N. . . . May Your most Precious Blood descend upon those suffering in Purgatory, and grant that their purification may be hastened, that so they may be counted worthy to rejoice with You in the Heavenly country."

At the PATER NOSTER:

"How great Your goodness in allowing me to call You Father, with what joy and what confidence this word inspires me. Yes, O God my Father, I am Your child; I trust in You.

"O Mary, our most merciful Mother, help me always to say this holy prayer, taught me by your Divine Son, with the most fervent devotion.

"O God, extinguish in my heart every feeling of jealousy, hatred and revenge, so that forgiving all who have offended me I may be pardoned by You.

"Keep all pride far from me; make me to truly know myself, that so I may always abide in true humility of heart. Grant me prudence so that I am ever on the watch against every temptation. Take from my heart every inordinate affection to created things. Deliver me from all evil, but especially from *the* evil of sin, which can separate me for ever from Your Adorable

Presence. St. Thérèse, help me and pray for me."

At the AGNUS DEI:

"O Lamb of God, who takest away the sins of the world, have mercy upon me and grant me Thy peace.

"O beloved little Saint, you had the precious grace of being preserved in your baptismal innocence, and always had the greatest horror of even the smallest fault. Obtain for me by your powerful intercession the grace desired above all others, that I may never fall into mortal sin, or if I should be so unhappy as to do so, that I may at once have recourse to the Sacrament of Reconciliation. May God's grace be with me all the days of my life to keep me from sin, to strengthen me to face all the hardships of this difficult journey towards eternity, that finally I may reach the harbour of everlasting salvation."

At the COMMUNION:

If you cannot receive Jesus sacramentally, make an act of spiritual communion, using some such words as the following:

"My adorable Jesus, although I cannot receive You sacramentally, I wish to receive You spiritually. Come to my heart and make it all Your own. Jesus, I am not worthy that You should enter within me, but speak the word, and my soul shall be healed.

"O beloved Mistress, you who in this world loved Jesus so passionately in this Sacrament of His Love, supply by your ardent love what is lacking in mine. May your profound humility, your angelic purity, your holy recollection and your burning love, proved by so many sacrifices and generous renunciations, supply for my unworthiness. O Thérèse of the Child Jesus, give me part in the living faith, the sure hope and the constant love which filled your heart towards Jesus in the Blessed Sacrament."

At the POST COMMUNION:

"He led her about and taught her and held her as the apple of His eye. Like as the eagle He has spread His wings and taken her and carried her upon His shoulders. The Lord alone was her Leader."

"O sweet Thérèse of the Child Jesus, all love and confidence, filled with the spirit of sacrifice, generous victim of love, would that I could offer a heart like yours to God. Deign to give thanks for me to the Lord for His manifold mercies which have followed me all the days of my life. Through your potent intercession before the great white throne send down a rain of roses upon that multitude of souls who are in such grievous need upon earth. Help me to follow the path of spiritual childhood in humility and self-effacement, in sacrifice and love, and keep far from me all that may endanger the peace and safety of my soul. Keep me in peace and love. May I live in Him who is my true happiness in time, and my sure hope for eternity."

At the LAST PRAYER:

"O Lord, may this divine mystery inflame us with that Heavenly fire of love by which Thy Blessed Virgin Saint Thirese offered herself a victim of love for souls. Through Our Lord Jesus Christ Thy Son, who with Thee liveth and reigneth in the unity of the Holy Ghost for ever and ever. Amen."

"O my most sweet Mother Mary Immaculate, who came to smile upon your child Thérèse at the dawn of her life, surrounding her with the most tender love, allow me like her to be your loving child. I commend myself to your most holy protection. It was in an agony of grief, sweet Mother, that you turned away from the sepulchre in which was laid the tortured body of your dearly loved Son. It is with grief, too, that I leave this altar where I have assisted at the Holy Sacrifice. But, sweet Mother, while you left Calvary your head remained united to

Jesus, and I, too, would remain united to Him.

"O Jesus, grant that I may know something of that holy intimacy with You which Your holy little spouse, St. Thérèse, experienced."

At the BLESSING:

"O most piteous Jesus, bless me with a benediction like that which You bestowed upon Your sweet Mother Mary, and may the fruit of this Holy Sacrifice be with me all the days of my life."

At the LAST GOSPEL:

"Sweet little Mistress, you who loved Jesus so much, especially in this most wonderful sacrament, may these moments which I have spent before the Altar bring forth fruit unto life eternal. Send down your roses from Heaven according to your promise and help me in all my necessities."

After MASS: "O Almighty Everlasting God, I give thanks to Your Divine Majesty for the favour You have granted me of assisting at this Holy Sacrifice, when so many others who have wished to do so have not been able. Forgive my want of fervour and recollection and increase in my soul love and gratitude. May this adorable Sacrifice avail to cleanse me of past faults, sanctify me in the present, and give assurance of eternal glory in the future. St. Thérèse of the Child Jesus, pray for me."

The Holy Sacrifice of the Mass is the mystery of Redeeming Love, the one Eternal Sacrifice of the Lamb slain from the foundation of the world, not another sacrifice, not a repetition, but the same Sacrifice.

Just as it is the same sun which sets in the evening that rises again in the morning, so, too, is this the same Sacrifice as that of Calvary. If I could step off this earth into space I should see no rising and setting of the sun, but see it shining always in its strength without variation. So, too, if I could step from time to eternity I should see the Sacrifice of Calvary as one single Eternal Act without shadow of variation; the Sacrifice of Calvary and the Sacrifice of the Mass one selfsame Sacrifice.

I repeat what I said at the beginning, these prayers are mere indications of the way in which to speak in prayer to God and His saints in order to help souls to learn to converse with God lovingly and with simplicity of heart. Some souls need no words to express their love, reverence and devotion, others need words in which to clothe their aspirations, but however this may be it is the loving, reverent adoration of the heart for which God looks. If we are intensely in love with Jesus it will not be difficult to find the way in which to express our love.

CHAPTER VIII
HOLY COMMUNION WITH ST. THÉRÈSE

꒰᯽꒱

THE intense love of St. Thérèse towards Jesus in the Blessed Sacrament is manifested alike in her prose and her verse.

With what eagerness as a little girl she desired to receive Jesus, so much so that one day when out walking it was with difficulty that she was restrained from running up to the Bishop as he was passing, and imploring him to let her make her first Communion at once instead of having to wait until she had completed her eleventh year, as was then the rule. Although she did not live to see the obstructions removed which kept children away from this life-giving Sacrament, we are assured that her prayers in Heaven obtained from the Heart of God this favour which she had so ardently desired for herself.

Her other desire was for the restoration of daily Communion, a desire which was accorded by Pius X not long after her death.

Except for the period of the great sickness in the convent during 1891, she never herself had the happiness of daily Communion, but always longed for the day when daily Communion should become general; and not long before her death, in a conversation with her eldest sister Marie, she uttered a prophecy which was fulfilled a fortnight after her death. After referring to the suffering she had endured on account of this privation, she continued:

"But it will not always be thus. A time will come when perhaps the Abbé Hodierne will be our chaplain and he will give us Holy Communion every day."

"Why do you think the Abbé Hodierne will be our chaplain?" "I hope that he will come, and that we shall be very happy with him."

In fact, by October 15 following he was already appointed and delivered his first conference to the sisters, taking for his text the words, "Come and eat my Bread"; words which thrilled with joy the hearts of his hearers.

How well our little Mistress realized the reason for the presence of Jesus in our midst. "It is not to rest in the golden Ciborium that He descends each day from Heaven, but that He may find another heaven, the heaven of our souls, in which He may take His delight."

How wonderfully, too, has she pictured the great day so eagerly expected of her first Communion:

"At last there dawned the most beautiful day of all the days of my life. How well I remember even the smallest details of those sacred moments! The joyful awakening, the reverent and tender embraces of our mistresses and older companions, the room filled with white frocks, like so many snowflakes where each child was dressed in turn, and above all our entrance into the chapel and the melody of the morning hymn: 'O Altar of God, over which angels are hovering.' But I would not and could not tell all. There are things which lose their fragrance when exposed to the air, and our most intimate thoughts cannot be translated into the language of earth without at once losing their deep and heavenly significance. Ah! how sweet was that first kiss of Jesus to my soul. Yes, it was a kiss of love! I felt I was loved, and said: 'I love You and give myself to You for ever!' Jesus asked nothing of me, claimed no sacrifices. For a long time already He and little Thérèse had known and understood each other. But our meeting on this day was more than a simple glance, it was a fusion. We were no longer two; Thérèse had disappeared like a drop of water lost in the immensity of the ocean."

Our little Saint well understood the immensity of the gift which comes to us in Holy Communion—nothing less than our adorable Jesus Himself in all the Almightiness of His Divinity, in all the strength of His Humanity. He comes with His Infinite love and grace, and she realized the marvellous union of the creature and the Creator which takes place at the moment of Holy Communion.

Now let us make our preparation, Holy Communion and thanksgiving in company with her. She will teach us and help us to love our Jesus as she loved Him.

PREPARATION

Let us ask her first of all to help us to make a good preparation.

"O most sweet spouse of Jesus, how ardently your heart was burning with love as you went to meet Jesus in the Blessed Sacrament. How eagerly you desired that each heart should continually love, praise and adore Him; that each soul might be filled with grace and adorned with virtue so that our Jesus at His coming might find a fitting tabernacle in which to dwell. Come beside me, little Mistress, and help me so that I may receive Him holily, reverently and profitably. Inflame my heart and my will with the most ardent affection, so that daily receiving my adorable Jesus in Holy Communion I may grow in grace, increase in sanctity, and so make a straight way to the

85

heavenly country."

Act of Humility. "My most sweet adorable Jesus, what follies have I not run after. With what foolish blindness have I despised Your Infinite Majesty, how forgetful I have been of Your Infinite Goodness. How easily I have been fascinated by the glittering vanities of earth. My Jesus, how many souls have been eternally lost who have offended You far less than I? My adorable Saviour, You have poured forth the precious tide of Your Blood for my salvation, and alas! how little I have valued Your immense love and incomparable mercy. But now, my adorable Jesus, I return to You, have pity upon me, cleanse my soul from every stain in Your Precious Blood. Enlighten me with Your presence, confirm me in Your Grace, set my heart aflame with love.

"Come, my adorable Jesus, come to my heart and make it Your home! Yes, make it Your home, although I am so utterly undeserving of this immense favour. Do you, my loving little Mistress Thérèse, obtain for me something of the love and affection with which you welcomed Jesus to your heart when you were upon earth."

Act of Contrition. "O Jesus, my most loving Redeemer, blot out all my sins in Your Blood, may that Blood cleanse me and wash away every stain. I detest my sins, which have pierced Your Divine Heart, I hate my inexpressible ingratitude, not because by my sins I have deserved Hell with all its torments, but because they have grieved and wounded You, my most sweet Love.

"O Thérèse, my Heavenly Patroness, through your purity and the horror you had of the least stain of sin, plead for me with Jesus, whom you received with such marvellous love and affection."

Act of Faith. "With the most profound Adoration in the

presence of Your Divine Majesty I firmly profess and believe all that You have revealed, all that Your Church proposes or shall propose for my belief, and for this faith I am ready to die; especially I believe in Your true real substantial presence in this Holy Sacrament as surely as if I behold You visibly present with the eyes of my flesh.

"I offer You, my Jesus, the perfect faith of Your Immaculate Mother, and that of Your Thérèse, who, in the blackest darkness, never faltered and held fast to You with unbounded confidence in Your goodness and mercy.

"My Jesus, I believe: increase my faith. Give me a living faith which expresses itself not in word only but in deed and in truth."

Act of Hope. "O God of Infinite Power and Majesty, I hope all things from Your Infinite Goodness. Through the Infinite merits of Your Divine Son, through His Blood shed upon Calvary, through His precious Death and Passion, I hope for forgiveness of all my sins, grace to overcome every temptation, and the enjoyment of the blessed face-to-face vision of Yourself in the heavenly country.

"O sweet little Mistress, who hoped against hope and gave such a wonderful example of unceasing confidence in the thick darkness which enveloped you, obtain for me from the Heart of God the gift of a living hope which shall vanquish all my fears.'

Act of Love. "God is Love! To love You, O God, and be loved by You, this is fullness of joy both in time and in eternity. How well Your sweet child Thérèse understood this mystery of Love, how this love inspired her with courage amidst all the conflicts of earth, and how it inspires her still in her great apostolate for souls.

"My sweet Jesus, I would love You as Your beloved little

Thérèse loved You. Come, come, my most adorable Jesus, come to my, heart. My Jesus, I love You! You know that I love You: Jesus, come, come, despite all my misery and wretchedness, come to my heart. I offer to You my sweetest love, all the love of Your Immaculate Mother, all the love of Your Thérèse, all the love of all Your angels and saints. Come, Jesus, and live in me. Amen."

Act of Desire. "My adorable Redeemer, my first Love, my only Love, You are my Jesus and my all, my life, my salvation, my love, my joy, my all. Jesus, come and inflame my heart, set it on fire with Your Love! May this fire consume all the stains of sin, all my faults and failings: come, my supreme, my only Good. May this Heavenly fire consume me wholly and transform me into Itself.

"O beloved little Mistress, Thérèse of the Child Jesus, how wonderful was your love of Jesus in this most adorable Sacrament, obtain for me a love like yours, that our Jesus when He comes may find my heart aflame with love and eager desire.

"Jesus! Jesus! Jesus! Divine Son! Light of Life, Light of Love, come, renew my soul, make her white in the scarlet of Your Blood. Lamb of God who takest away the sins of the world, come and reign in my heart, make it Your throne, make it, although so unworthy, Your home. I am not worthy for You to enter my heart, but yet, Jesus, speak but one word and I shall be clean, speak but one word and I shall be made worthy with Your own worthiness. My Jesus, come, I love You, You know I love You. Amen."

THANKSGIVING

"O Jesus, Thou art all mine; I am all Thine. I give myself wholly to You, all that I have and am is Yours, now and for all eternity.

"My sweet adorable Jesus, a thousand thousand welcomes! Sweet Jesus, a thousand thousand thanks for Your immense Goodness in coming to my poor heart.

"I adore, I bless, I praise You. Now it is no longer I who live, but You who live in me. O Joy of Heaven come down to Earth! O Jesus, henceforth do with me as You please and I shall be pleased with what You do. What You love I love. What You hate I hate. What pleases You pleases me, I *abandon* myself entirely to Your Good Pleasure, do with me as You will.

"Grant me, my adorable Jesus, perfect purity of heart and conscience, make me humble and patient, sweet and gracious. Grant that all my words, thoughts and actions may be pleasing to You. Increase the fire of love within me so that I burn with love for You, and love all in You and for You.

"O adorable and ever Blessed Trinity, Father, Son and Holy Ghost, I adore, I love and give thanks to You for Your great glory.

"Eternal Father, You have so loved the world as to give Your Sole Begotten Son for its ransoming, I give thanks to You for Your Infinite Goodness.

"Eternal Son of the Eternal Father, God made man, Divine Victim for my redemption, the one all-sufficient sacrifice for all the sins of all the world. I adore You, I praise and bless You for Your infinite love and mercy and desire to love and praise You eternally. Amen. Jesus, give me a heart like that of Your beloved St. Thérèse, give me a love like hers with which to love You.

"O Holy Spirit, Spirit of Love, come and kindle in my heart the fire of Your Love.

"O Eternal Father, Almighty Everlasting God, I offer all the praise and thanksgiving which Your Divine Son offered to You throughout His earthly life, especially at the moment in which He instituted this most Adorable Sacrament.

"I offer the adoration of His most sweet Mother which she offered to You when she uttered that *Fiat* through which the Eternal Word became flesh and dwelt amongst us, I offer the adoration of all the angels and saints, and especially of Your loving child and victim St. Thérèse, whose heart thrilled with such fervent love for You in this Sacrament of Your Love."

Act of Offering: "O God, Infinite in Goodness: I praise and adore You for bestowing the gift of Your Grace upon me. Jesus, You have loved me and given Yourself for me upon the Altar of the Cross, and You come to give me Yourself in this adorable Sacrament. I offer myself, all I am and have to be Your possession, wholly Yours to do with as You will.

"I renew the vows of my baptism, and the desires and promises I have ever made of loving, serving and adoring You. Grant, my most adorable Jesus, that this heart in which You are dwelling at this moment may never be drawn away after the vain things of earth. May You, my sweetest Jesus, be absolute Lord and Master, may my love for You increase with each breath I draw until finally liberated from the body I may be one with You eternally in Heaven.

"O glorious St. Thérèse, pray for me that henceforth I may live in Jesus, and Jesus may live in me. May His immense love fill my soul and transform me into Himself."

Act of Love: "My love, my all, I love You and desire nought but Your love alone. Despise not the voice of my supplication, but hearken and do with me after Your great goodness and the multitude of Your mercies. Amend my many faults. Jesus, my sweet Love, You know my frailty, be my strength ; when my foot slips hold me up in the strong arms of Your love ; when the fascinations of this world allure me, open my eyes to their vanity, when the Fiend of Hell assails me, thrust him down to the pit whence he came ; give me grace to tread underfoot the world, the flesh and the Devil.

"May each heart-beat be all for You. Keep me free from the contamination of sin ; keep me pure and chaste amidst all the seductions of earth, protect and help me with Your grace all the days of my pilgrimage, and when exile is over grant me a blessed entrance into Your Heavenly Kingdom.

"O Jesus, meek and humble of heart, make my heart like unto Yours.

"Soul of Christ sanctify me, Body of Christ save me, Blood of Christ inebriate me, water from the side of Christ wash me. Passion of Christ strengthen me. O good Jesus, hear me. Within Your wounds hide me. Never permit me to be separated from You. From the malignant enemy defend me. In the hour of my death call me, and bid me come to You that with Your Saints I may praise You to endless ages. Amen.

"O most Adorable Saviour, by Your bitter Cross and Passion, by Your death and burial, by Your glorious and triumphant Resurrection give me victory over my enemies, and grant me to have part with You in Your everlasting Kingdom where I may love, praise and adore You everlastingly.

"I commend to Your infinite mercy all near and dear to me, in particular all those united with me in the Pious Union of Your Thérèse, together with all who have desired my prayers, and grant us all a place in Your Heavenly Kingdom at the last. Grant to all the faithful departed eternal rest, everlasting happiness and the face-to-face vision of Yourself.

"Most glorious and Immaculate Virgin Mary, plead for me and all mine before the great White Throne. St. Joseph, intercede for me. My Guardian Angel, protect me. St. Thérèse of the Child Jesus, pray for me. Amen."

"May Jesus Christ be praised every moment in the most adorable Sacrament of the Altar.

"Jesus, hold me to Your Heart in life and in death. I love You, I love You, I love You. Amen. Amen."

These thoughts will give you an idea how to speak to Jesus before and after Holy Communion. When you leave your place to go to the altar do not genuflect on leaving your seat, but walk straight up to the altar-rails and then kneel down, holding your head slightly back at the moment of Communion, and do not incline or bend forward until the priest has left you and begun to say the words of administration to the one following you, then rise without genuflecting, and with hands joined before you return to your place in the church.

CHAPTER IX
CONFESSION WITH ST. THÉRÈSE

HERE is no Sacrament which sets forth the loving pity of God in such a wonderful way as the Sacrament of Penance, through which sins committed after Baptism are blotted out in the Blood of the Son of God.

The Eternal Son speaks the word of forgiveness through the lips of His earthly representative: I forgive you your sins, in the Name of the Father, of the Son and the Holy Ghost. Amen.

This truth was impressed vividly upon the mind of St. Thérèse by her sister Pauline when preparing for her first Confession: "My little Thérèse, it is not to a man, but to God Himself that you are going to confess your sins." "So fully was I persuaded of this truth," says St. Thérèse, "that I seriously asked if I ought to say to M. l'Abbé Ducellier, that I loved him with all my heart, seeing that it was to God I was speaking through his person.

"Well instructed as to all I had to do, I entered the confessional and knelt down; but when the priest opened the slide he saw no one, for I was so small that my head came beneath the elbow rest. He then bade me to stand up. I at once obeyed and turned myself towards him that I might see him better. I made my confession and received absolution in a spirit of most lively faith, for he assured me that at that moment the tears of little Jesus would purify my soul. I remember the exhortation which he addressed to me; how above all he urged me to be devout towards the Blessed Virgin; and how I resolved to redouble my love for her who already held so large a place in my heart. Finally, I passed him my rosary to bless, and came out of the confessional feeling light-hearted and contented to an extent I had never known before. ... The influence of the grace I received remained with me for long after and henceforth I went to Confession for all the great feasts. These confessions, I may add, filled my young heart with transports of joy."

Two months after her entry into Carmel she made a general confession to Father Pichon, S. J., which brought her great consolation: "When I had finished he said: 'Before God, the Blessed Virgin, the Angels, and all Saints I declare you have never committed a mortal sin. You must thank God for this favour which He has freely bestowed upon you without any merit on your part.'

'Without any merit on my part! I had no difficulty in believing that! I realized how feeble and imperfect I was, and my heart overflowed with gratitude. The fear of having stained the white robe of my baptism had caused me much suffering, and this assurance coming from the lips of a director such as our Holy Mother Teresa desired—that is to say, one who combines knowledge with virtue—seemed to me to come from God Himself."

In the year after her profession a retreat was preached by one who had a greater reputation for converting sinners than perfecting saints, however, one whom God used to bring her much light and consolation.

"Previously," she says, "I had been a prey to all kinds of interior trials which I had found it impossible to make clearly known. But now I was able to unburden myself in a most marvellous way, so that the Father fully understood me and even divined the state of my soul. He launched me full sail upon the ocean of confidence and love which had long attracted me, but over which I had scarcely dared to venture. He told me my faults did not grieve God, and added, 'At this moment I who hold His place assure you on His behalf that He is well pleased with your soul.'

"How happy was I on hearing these consoling words! For I had never heard before it was possible that faults should not give pain to God. That assurance filled me with joy, and gave me patience to endure the exile of life. I had long felt that Our Lord is more tender than a mother, and I have fathomed the depths of more than one mother's heart. I know by sweet experience how ready a mother is to forgive the small involuntary faults of her child. No reproach could have touched me so much as one single kiss from you (her sister Pauline). My nature is such that fear makes me shrink, while with love I not only advance, but fly!"

Perhaps you will say that is all very well for St. Thérèse, who never knew mortal sin, but what in my case who have fallen grievously and often, what shall my attitude be towards God? Our little Mistress has herself supplied the answer:

"As soon as I open the Gospels I breathe the perfume exhaled by the life of Jesus, and know which way to run. It is not the highest place but the lowest to which I hasten. I leave the Pharisee to go forward, while full of confidence I repeat the humble prayer of the Publican. Above all I imitate the conduct of the Magdalen, for her amazing, rather her loving audacity which delighted the Heart of Jesus has cast its spell upon mine!

"It is not because I have been preserved from mortal sin that I lift up my heart to God in confidence and love. I feel

95

assured that had I upon my conscience every imaginable crime, I should lose nothing of my confidence. I should go heartbroken with repentance and throw myself into the arms of my Saviour. I recall His love for the prodigal son, I have heard His words to St. Mary Magdalen, to the woman taken in adultery, to the woman of Samaria. No, there is no one who can make me afraid, for I know too well what to believe concerning His Mercy and His Love, and I know that all that multitude of offences would vanish in the twinkling of an eye like a drop of water in a white-hot brazier."

There we have the dispositions with which we should go to confession: heart-broken sorrow for having sinned and grieved God, and complete confidence in His Infinite Love and Mercy.

The first step in preparing for confession is to know the truth about ourselves, to see ourselves as God sees us. Let us say to God along with our holy Mistress: "I implore You to answer me when I humbly ask, 'What is the truth?' Make me see things exactly as they are. Yes, Jesus, show me the exact truth about myself, in what I have offended You, how often, and how grievously!"

The frequency of confession will generally depend on the frequency of Communion, those who go to the altar every day will usually go to Confession once a fortnight. It is important in preparing one's confession to distinguish between sins and imperfections, between grave and venial sin.

The first stage then of preparation is to discover the exact truth about our state. Naturally, as a rule, those who frequently receive Jesus in the Blessed Sacrament will not have any grave sin to confess, but only those venial sins which it is difficult without special grace to entirely avoid. Now the essential purpose of the Sacrament of Penance is for the forgiveness of mortal sin, because it is one of the Sacraments of the dead, that is to say, one of the two Sacraments which restore the spiritually dead to life. If there is no mortal sin to confess, then a sin of one's past life must be mentioned, in order that there may be matter for Absolution, and then the soul receives an increase of grace through this Sacrament.

In the second place there is sorrow for sin! The more we love anyone the more we are grieved if we have hurt them, even inadvertently. The measure of our sorrow will be the measure of our love. It is true that God is more grieved by the slight faults of His friends, than by the more grievous sins of those who are far off from Him. Of course, the Disciples of St. Thérèse are those who are at least trying to love much, trying to love Jesus as she loved Him, and usually, for that very reason, they will feel a deeper grief over their lighter faults than others over more grievous sins. But no soul need despair, for, as our little Mistress has said, ardent love and confidence in God's mercy will find instant response from His Divine Heart, and she instances the story of the poor sinner who had led a life of shame, whose repentance was so intense that she died of grief on the first day of her journey to the desert to do penance. Love accomplished in a few hours what years of penance could not; and so it is still.

So tell Jesus how sorry you are, not from dread of punishment due to sin, but because you have grieved Him whom you love so much. Ask little Thérèse to come and help you to grieve over your sins as you ought.

Next, tell Jesus you are resolved never to offend Him again, but you know of yourself you will never be able to keep your resolve, because of yourself you can do nothing. Ask Jesus to give you His strength so that when the Devil comes you may overcome him. Then go to the Confessional and make your confession, and say how long it is since your last confession, then mention your sins, and approximately how many times you have fallen into each particular sin. Mention those which are more serious first, and the lesser afterwards. Do not mention a third person unless necessary to make the matter clear, and then, of course, never mention that person's name. Speak in a subdued voice, but one sufficiently clear for the priest to hear you. Avoid useless repetitions and telling the same story over and over again.

Now, as to the faults which are not sins, if you are seeking spiritual direction, you mention them, and if you have made a promise or vow to God to avoid certain defects, mention the fact, as otherwise the reason for confessing them will not be clear. Some souls need a great deal of direction, others very little. St. Thérèse never had what is called a spiritual director, and the Church sings of her that "God alone was her Leader." At the times when she needed light, God provided it through the ordinary confessor. The only one in whom she might have found a permanent director was Father Pichon, S. J., but soon after her coming to Carmel he was sent to Canada, and at best she could only look for a letter once a year. He said to her: "May Our Lord always be your superior and your novice-master!" "And, in fact," says St. Thérèse, "He has been my Director. Our Lord Himself has always been my Spiritual Guide."

Yet she did not undervalue spiritual direction, and realized its value for souls, but she also realized it was not well to lean too much upon support which at any time might be removed.

Over-direction produces scrupulosity, and frequently results in a soul not daring to do the simplest thing without permission of the director. It is better that the director and confessor should be the same person, unless there are exceptional reasons to the contrary.

Having completed your confession, listen attentively to the advice God gives you through the confessor, and then, as the priest pronounces the Absolution, make the Act of Contrition in some such words as these: "O Jesus, I am so sorry I have offended You because You are so good. With Your help I will never sin again."

Then go back to your place in the church and say the penance which the confessor has imposed, and turn with loving confidence to Jesus, tell Him how much you love Him and how you desire to do all you can to please Him in the future and make amends for the past. Speak to Him naturally with the loving simplicity of a child, saying something like this:

"My adorable Jesus, how infinitely good and merciful You are to me who have grieved You so much by my stupidity and folly. You have forgiven me and taken me back again to Your Heart. How sorry I am, how I hate myself for all the grief I have caused You. I do not deserve Your forgiveness I know full well, but You are so loving and compassionate that You have blotted out all my sins in Your Blood. Jesus, may I never offend You again. Give me Your strength; come live within me, then I shall not fail or falter in the fight. Jesus, You know I love You, and want to do all I can to prove my love by deeds. Amen.

Sweet little Thérèse, obtain for me from Jesus the grace to be faithful unto death, and never to hurt Him any more."

CHAPTER X
HERE AND NOW

E are at war, and at war with an enemy who is a past-master in all the strategy of war. This enemy is the Devil, and we must never leave him out of account, for if we do we shall have good reason to rue our folly. The good soldier is always on his guard even when he sleeps; he sleeps with his arms in his hands so that sudden attack may not take him by surprise. "Be sober and vigilant," says St. Peter, "because your adversary the Devil goes about as a roaring lion seeking whom he may devour."

Now the Devil has one very favourite mode of attack, and suggests: "If only you were in a different place and different surroundings, if only you were engaged in different work, and if only you had different companions, then you could really do something for God, but in this place, with these people, and with this particular work you cannot serve God as you desire."

The Devil's great aim is to push off the serving of God to some distant future, which will never eventuate, and if he succeeds in persuading the soul to think thus, has already half won the battle. It is a very insidious form of attack, because it uses our present work, place and companions as an excuse for coldness and indifference in God's service.

Now we must realize that place, work, surroundings are three things which do not matter, because we can serve God anywhere; there is no place, no work, no surroundings in which we may not give glory to God.

And this particular mode of attack is repeated again and again, in a slightly varied form each time, it is true, but always essentially unchanged, for the Devil's objective is ever the same, to prevent our giving God the adoration, love and service which we should be giving Him at this moment. The attack may be beaten off, and the Devil may retire—for a season—but he will return to the attack when a more favourable occasion presents itself.

First, there is the question of place. The particular part of the town or country in which I have to live is so depressing or uninteresting, that I always long to get away to some other place, which—for distance always lends enchantment to the view—would be so delightful, and where my health would be better, in fact, where everything would be better.

The answer to the temptation is this: This is the particular part of the battle-front on which God wills me to fight; after all, I am a stranger and pilgrim in this world, I am only here for a while, and what does it matter if the city or country is beautiful and interesting or not—I am going to hold on here, stand my ground and fight.

Second, there is my work. It is so tiresome, so fatiguing, so depressingly uninteresting. Now if I were engaged in work into which I could put my whole heart, I should be able to give it all to God, but here I am so sick and tired of it all that it is quite impossible, always the same year in and year out.

But it is just because the work is so uninteresting, so tiring, so depressing that I can give more to God than if it were of a more attractive character. Here and now I am going to do this work, this day in this place all for Jesus, I am going to offer it all to Him; then how different it becomes. Once I realize that Jesus has so disposed things that this is the particular work He has given me to do here and now, then the most wearisome work becomes a pleasure, not in itself, but for love of Him for whom I am doing it.

Finally there are those with whom we have to associate, those with whom we have to live. Some are difficult to get on with, they are full of complaints, whatever we do they are never satisfied, and of course the Devil says no wonder you can't serve God, living with these impossible people with their everlasting grumblings morning, noon and night. And he brings before us a vision of another place that is so delightful, of other work which is so pleasant, and finally of other companions who are all so kindly and gracious, and then he contrasts this with our life just as it is, and says: "See how happy and well off others are, what charming friends and companions they have, everything is there to make life possible and God's service easy." Yes, our companions, those we live with, are difficult! But what then? We must follow our little Mistress, who always went out of her way to do some act of kindness for difficult characters, and by her sweet smile and gracious manner won their hearts. That must be our way. Here in this place, at this work, with these people I am going to give Jesus everything, for it is only when I have made the complete oblation of everything that I really begin to experience the joy and liberty of the children of God.

The Devil will return to the attack, but each time he will be beaten off, if I keep in mind that God has set me here, given me this work and these companions as the means by which to save my soul and give Him glory.

This mirage, for such it is, of a future in which we shall be able to love and serve God is one with which the Devil assails every state and condition in the Church, priests and religious are no more exempt from it than are the faithful. The Devil attacks the priest by showing how little he is doing in the place to which he has been sent, and suggests that the only hope of really doing anything for God is to go somewhere else; if the Devil gains the advantage once, he will pursue it, and exploit it to the full, for wherever the priest goes the tempter will be there with the same temptation, and so we see priests continually on the move, no sooner in one place than they want to be in another.

The same temptation comes to religious; another house and they will be all right, another order, another kind of work, other surroundings, other religious and then they will be able to serve God perfectly. How crafty the Devil is, what a master in the art of war!

Thus we find priests, religious and faithful all attacked in exactly the same way, and if they give way to the first attack of the Devil, he will come the same way again and again until a lifetime slips away in useless dreaming of a future which never comes, they move from place to place, change from work to work, always with the same result; after a few weeks the new place, the new work, the new surroundings lose their charm, and the Devil scores another victory; never once do these unfortunate souls come down to reality, because they are ever following a mirage which always recedes as they approach it.

How many tragedies of the spiritual life are due to this deadly delusion! How many!

The only moment we can ever have in which to love and serve God is the present moment: "*Now* is the appointed time, *now* is the day of salvation." "This is the day which the Lord has made," this day. We must give Jesus everything now at this very moment, and go on giving Jesus everything in all the succeeding moments till the last moment of all.

How well St. Augustine, in the tremendous struggle at the time of his conversion, realized this fact! "Tomorrow, tomorrow," said the tempter. But God said now, and grace triumphed.

"Today if you will hear His voice." St. Thérèse realized the supreme importance of living in the present moment and in her song of today insists on it very strongly:

My life is but an instant, only a passing hour.
My life is a moment which escapes me and is gone.
You know it, O my God, that to love You upon this earth
I have only today.
O how I love You, Jesus, to You my soul aspires.
For one day only come and be my sweet support.
Come, reign in my heart, give me your smile just for today.
What matters it if the future be sombre,
do I pray for tomorrow, no, that I cannot do.
Keep my heart pure, cover me with Thy wings
Just for today.
If I dream of tomorrow, my inconstancy I fear,
I feel begotten in my heart sadness and ennui.
But well I know, my God, that suffering and trial
Are only for today.

Our hopes and our fears about the future only distract us from the living present. Now is the acceptable time, now. This day I must give Jesus everything, live each instant as it passes all for Him. This day is the day which the Lord has made for *me,* every joy and sorrow, every pain, every gain, all that happens in it He has foreseen from all eternity. He could have changed each happening, arrested each blow, I could have been in another place, I could have been engaged on other work, I could have lived amongst other people, but He has so disposed things that I am here, in this place, at this work, with these

105

people. Here, then, it is that I must give Him glory, this is the work I must do for Him, these are the people amongst whom I must live.

"There are people," says St. Thérèse, "who take everything in the way which gives them the most trouble. With me it is the reverse; I always try to see the best side of things. If I have nought but pure suffering without relief, well, then, I make it my joy."

How many people take everything that befalls them in the worst way possible! They are full of complaints about their hard lot, nothing pleases them, everyone has said or done something which upsets them, they never have a good word for anyone or anything. All because they have taken the wrong way, and have listened to the Devil, who has a wonderful way of making us see things in the worst possible light.

St. Thérèse speaking of a sister who was such a trial to her said: "The Devil must have had something to do with it, for undoubtedly it was he who made me see so many disagreeable points in her character. I would not yield to the natural antipathy which I experienced, and reminded myself that charity should not be a mere sentiment, but prove itself by deeds, so I endeavoured to treat this sister as I should my most cherished friend. . . . I did not rest satisfied with praying earnestly for her who had given me occasion for so many combats, but I tried to render her as many services as possible, and when tempted to make a disagreeable answer, I always hastened to smile and change the conversation. . . The outcome of all this was that one day she said to me with a radiant countenance: 'Tell me, Sister Thérèse, what it is which you find so attractive in me? I never meet you without being welcomed by your most gracious smile.'"

There our little Mistress shows us how to act when we

meet with difficult people, for however difficult they may be, a loving smile wins in the end; even when their conduct seems blameworthy—perhaps if we could see them as God sees them we should see they were not really to blame at all.

Live wholly concentrated on the duty of the moment. This *is* what Jesus wants of me now. If I thus live in the present moment, the most difficult work is finished in far less time than I could dare expect. Living in the now, we anticipate the Eternal now of Heaven, for the joy of Heaven is this; there is no past or future, but only one glorious present in which is the fullness of all things possessed all at once with perfect possession.

Tomorrow when it comes will be today; and by living in the present moment and loving Jesus and desiring nothing to be other than it is, we give Him that pleasure which is the sole reason of our creation.

And we have joys as well as sorrows, moments of gladness as well as moments of distress, because Eternal Wisdom mightily and sweetly disposing all things has willed that there should be moments when we seem to anticipate the joy of Heaven. True, they pass all too quickly and are gone, but they strengthen the soul in her combat with the powers of darkness.

But no matter how hard the fight may be, we must always retain a quiet and joyful spirit. "The soul," says our little Mistress, "is reflected in the countenance; like a little child who is always content, your countenance should always be calm and serene. When you are alone, be still the same because you are ever in the angels' sight." It is not by changing our place, our work or surroundings that we shall better serve God, but by living wholly for Him *now*, and using our place, work, and surroundings to the best advantage by offering them all to Him.

"Rejoice in the Lord, and again I say rejoice," says the Apostle, and our adorable Jesus speaking to His Apostles said, "that your joy may be full," those very Apostles who were going to face persecution and death; how well they realized it when, after being cruelly scourged, they left the Council Chamber rejoicing that they were counted worthy to suffer for His sake!

CHAPTER XI
IN THE WORLD BUT NOT OF IT

E are in the world but not of it, like soldiers in an enemy country who must be continually on the watch lest they be surprised by the foe. The world was, is, and always will be the enemy of God; for "friendship with the world is enmity against God," and we know that "the whole world lieth in the arms of the wicked one."

We must look well at this world with which we are at war, the more so because some are inclined to think the world of today is a less dangerous foe than it was in the days of the Apostles. But the truth is the exact opposite of this, for the neo-pagan world of today which has thrown off the yoke of Christ has neither the morality of Christ or that of the ancient pagans. Everything which we hold sacred and holy it holds as evil, all that we hold as evil it holds as sacred: there is no room for compromise, it is war till the death. No, there can be no compromise with the world because the Saviour has come on earth not to bring peace but a sword. Let us lay to heart those words of our little Leader and never forget them: "We *must* fight in order that God may give us the victory."

War involves continual hardships and many sacrifices, and there are moments of war-weariness which are very favourable to the Devil. It is hard to always go against the tide, to be always taking a different side to that of those in whose midst we live, and the Devil is always at hand to suggest some pleasant compromise between Light and Darkness. But if we are true to our King we must go against the tide and not with it. Outside the Catholic Church religion disintegrates rapidly on every side, and the moral sanctions which centuries of Christian Faith have built up are everywhere being abandoned, only the Catholic Church stands as a strong rock amidst the flood.

Every Catholic is a soldier, and a soldier is bound to fight for his king and be true to him till death; this is true of Catholics in general, but it is especially true of those who have enrolled themselves as disciples of St. Thérèse, who have promised: "To observe the greatest purity in their conduct so as not to offend the Heavenly glance of our Saint as she looks down upon them. Women and young girls inscribed in this pious union must strictly observe the principles of Christian modesty in their dress in accordance with the repeated directions of the Church and the instant commands of the Pope and the bishops."

Now the disciples of St. Thérèse can never be the slaves of fashion when, as is so often the case, it offends the elementary principles of Christian decency. Look at those women who go about with painted lips, painted eyelashes, painted eyebrows, distended eyes in imitation of the half-witted gaze of some vulgar film star, painted finger-nails, painted toe-nails; not for a moment can the follower of St. Thérèse imitate these in their vanity and stupidity. In the very young, led away so easily by the seductions of the world and so ready to imitate, the light-headedness of youth may explain but not excuse; but what of those of middle age, and even older, to whom increase of years has only brought increase of folly. "Turn away mine eyes lest they behold vanity" is the prayer that must be ever upon the lips of the disciples of St. Thérèse, for beholding vanity how easy to be seduced by it. This is the snare by which the Devil seeks to allure innocent souls who are so quickly bewitched by the fascinations of the moment. "To do exactly as others do and not be singular" is the favourite advice of the Father of Lies, and he continues: "After all, vanity is not a sin, or if it is, it is not a very serious one."

These things are the outward expression of the neo-pagan revolt of which they are the more obvious manifestation. There is another which goes further. In how many seaside resorts men and women lie about the day long in a state of almost complete nudity, without the least regard for elementary decency. Even Catholics are led away by the flood, and what is worse, attempt to enter the church for Divine Worship in such a state. Have they so much as an elementary notion of the Divine Majesty into whose presence they come? Would they dare enter the presence chamber of an earthly king in such a guise? Here dwells no earthly ruler, but the King of Kings from whom all earthly rulers derive alike their authority and existence.

Again and again the Church has forbidden the admission of both men and women to the House of God when not becomingly attired. The most ordinary sense of reverence should suffice to prevent anyone bearing the Christian name from presenting themselves before the Most High in such attire, or rather, want of it.

The disciples of St. Thérèse will first of all avoid consenting in any way to such things, use all their influence to prevent others from doing so, and dress themselves in a way which becomes Christians, whether this involves being in fashion or not. Better be out of fashion in time, than in eternity. Again, there are cinemas and theatres which it is impossible to

111

frequent without injury to Christian purity and modesty; where all morality is held up to scorn, where vice and immorality in their worst aspects are glorified and held up for admiration.

How can anyone with a pure conscience frequent these places and not be defiled? How not gradually find their sense of Christian purity blunted by continually beholding its opposite? The neo-pagan world utterly rejects Christian morality and purity, chastity it regards as a crime, and the full indulgence of the passions as good and right, and their restraint wrong. Hence the Devil works through the theatre, but especially through the cinema, to defile souls, especially the souls of the young and innocent. He has no more effective weapon with which to wage war than that of the cinema.

Then there is the question of literature: the novel first of all, the modern novel which wallows in the mire of vice and sensuality. Here, again, who can read these things and not be defiled? Gradually but surely the moral sense is deadened, vice which at first appeared revolting, by constant representation becomes normal, accepted as the ordinary standard of life, and almost, without the soul being aware of it, the whole foundation of Christian morality has been shaken. It is this gradual process which is so insidious, because the effect produced by reading is one of which the reader is unconscious, for he does not perceive he is being influenced until a moment arrives when some chance happening shows how far he has travelled. The reading of novel after novel in which immorality of every kind is taken as the ordinary standard of life, slowly but surely tells on the reader, until finally he comes to share the views of the writer. If good books can lift the soul up to Heaven, bad books can cast her down to Hell.

But you will be quite out of everything if you do not keep

up with all the latest novels which everybody is reading! Such is the Devil's argument.

"Have you read such a novel?" "No, and I do not intend to, I would not touch it with a barge-pole." This is the only reply for a Christian. We must dare to stand alone, totally indifferent as to what people may say or think about our attitude; the only thing which matters is what God thinks of it. We are a separate people, called out, apart and consecrated to God, hence we can never handle, touch or taste the poisonous vanities which the world and the Devil hold out to us.

There are other branches of literature which directly assail Christian faith, morality and philosophy; these are the Devil's direct means of attack, and they complete the work which the novel has so successfully begun.

The assumption in both cases is the same, that the Catholic religion and Catholic morality are out of date, something which to the "enlightened intellectualism" of the twentieth century is a relic of the past. But to the one and the other we oppose an absolute *non possumus.* We are children of the light, and can have no communion with the unfruitful works of darkness.

The follies of fashion which sin against Christian modesty and morality, the disfiguring of face and hands and feet with paint, the cinemas where morality is outraged and vice glorified, the books which directly or indirectly war against Faith and morality, all these things must be spurned by those who follow the sure way of the Saint of Lisieux. Every penny spent on these things is a penny given to the Devil to advance his kingdom and destroy souls.

Another peril—conversation! We cannot take part in conversation in which stories openly immoral or merely suggestive have place, for both set up a train of thought not easily stopped. St. Paul has spoken very bluntly indeed about those who do these things. We pray for a chaste mind in a chaste body, but we can only conserve both by unceasing vigilance. We are at war with the Devil, who is both strong and crafty, and we are always in danger of being surprised by some new move of our ghostly enemy. If of ourselves we are very weak, we have all the strength of God to help us, His Grace is sufficient for us, and with it we shall vanquish all the craft of Hell.

Even in her own day our holy little Mistress realized full well how perilous was the state of souls living in the world, and by how many dangers they were surrounded, and at that time neo-paganism was not yet born; if perilous, then it is tenfold more perilous now, and she will surely come to our aid in these days when we need her aid so much. "How great," she writes, "is my compassion for souls that perish. How easy it is to go astray amidst the world's seductive ways! Without doubt to one advanced in virtue, the sweetness which the world offers is always mingled with bitterness, nor can the immense void of such a soul's desire be satisfied by the flatteries of a moment. But in my case, had not my heart been lifted up to God from its first awakening, had the world smiled on me from the cradle, there is no knowing what I might have become. How gratefully do I sing 'the mercies of the Lord,' for has He not, according to the word of Holy Wisdom, 'taken me away from the world lest wickedness should change my understanding or deceit beguile my soul.'"

Like our holy Mistress, while keeping ourselves unspotted from the world we must have the most tender pity for those who are carried away by its fascinating allurements. How easy it is, especially for the young, to be deceived and swept off their feet before being fully aware of what is happening. How

114

many souls, simple and upright, are deceived by the fleeting vanities of the moment.

By prayer, by word, but, above all, by example, the disciples of St. Thérèse must do all they can to save them. By prayer, because it overcomes every obstacle and brings grace to souls in most desperate need. The apostolate of prayer is within the reach of all. Then when we can speak a word which may be effective we must do so, but before and above all the example of our daily life must be such that they may "take knowledge of us that we have been with Jesus."

Actions speak louder than words, and the best apostolate of all is the apostolate of a consistent life lived in the power of the Son of God. "Love not the world," wrote the Apostle of Love, "nor the things which are in the world. ... For all that is in the world is the concupiscence of the flesh, the concupiscence of the eyes, and the pride of life, which is not of the Father but the world."

Our lot may be cast "even where Satan's seat is," but even there the grace of God is with us, and will bring us victoriously through the conflict. St. Thérèse relates a dream she had which encouraged her, and may well encourage us. She saw in her dream two hideous little devils, who at first cast fiery glances at her, but then suddenly fled and tried to hide from her, and finally scurried into the laundry. Seeing they were so afraid of her she went to look through the window; here she saw them racing about in a vain attempt to escape from her gaze. She comments on it thus: "I believe Our Lord made use of this to show me that a soul in a state of grace has nothing to fear from the Devil, who is a coward, and will fly even from the gaze of a little child." These words are an echo of St. Paul: "Resist the Devil and he will flee from you." There are moments when the world seems very strong, overbearing, arrogant and almost irresistible, and the Devil throws all his strength upon the soul in a desperate attempt to break down her resistance. At such a moment we may well recall that incident.

CHAPTER XII
THE MARRIED STATE AND ITS SACRIFICIAL CHARACTER

HE majority of those enrolled in the Association of the Disciples of St. Thérèse are called to serve God in the married state; called, because the married state is as much a vocation as the religious state, and especially in these days is not less sacrificial, as we shall see later on. St. Thérèse never entertained the narrow idea that sanctity was only attainable in the cloister, for she well knew that we *can* become saints anywhere, and that we attain sanctity by following the call of God and serving Him in the place which He has chosen for us, and not in that which we would choose for ourselves. Our little Mistress has made this very clear in a prayer which she wrote for one living in the world: "My God, to You I offer all the actions of today, for the intentions and glory of the Sacred Heart of Jesus. I wish to sanctify each beating of my heart, each thought, my simplest acts by uniting them to its infinite merits, and I wish to make amends for my sins by casting them into the furnace of its merciful love.

"O my God, I ask for myself and those dear to me the grace to fulfil *perfectly* Your Holy Will, and to accept for Your Love the joys and sorrows of this transitory life, that so one day we may be united together in Heaven for all eternity. Amen."

No small part of the universal apostolate of the Saint of

Lisieux is that of setting before the world a wonderful picture of the married state. In her Autobiography our little Mistress has shown us a family supernaturalized by grace, in which reigns a holy, joyous simplicity and loving affection such as the blind followers of the world can never know. St. Thérèse was the youngest in a family which counted nine children, and we come to know her better when we see the atmosphere of love, natural and supernatural, in which she was reared.

Both her parents felt called to the religious state, her father sought admission into the monastery of St. Bernard in the Alps, and her mother applied to the Sisters of St. Vincent de Paul in Alençon. But when it was made clear to both that such was not God's Will for them, there was no impatient haste to enter the married state, instead they remained for years seeking light from God by prayer (in the case of M. Martin, no less than fifteen) as to whom their future companion in life was to be.

Marie-Zélie Guerin, her mother, daily made this prayer to God: "Since I am not worthy to be Your bride Like my sister (a Visitation nun at Le Mans) I shall embrace the married state in fulfilment of Your Will. I pray You to give me many children, who may *all* be consecrated to You"; her prayer was fulfilled, for all her children became religious with the exception of the four who died in childhood.

There was something mysterious in the coming together of these two, for one day as she was crossing the Pont de St. Leonard she encountered a young man whose grave and distinguished bearing could not escape her observation. Although she was quite unacquainted with him, an interior voice said to her:

"This is he whom I have prepared for you." Those words ultimately brought them together, and on July 15 in the year 1858 they were married in the Church of Notre Dame at

Alençon.

They set up their home in the rue Pont-Neuf, where M. Martin established his business of jeweller, while his wife continued to carry on the making of the famous "point d'Alençon" lace which she had begun before marriage. In 1871 he was able to retire from business and take up his residence in the the rue Saint-Blaise, in which house St. Thérèse was born.

Sunday was especially devoted to the worship of God, and the favourite recreation on these days was reading of the Lives of the Saints. Their daily prayers were said together, a custom handed down from M. Martin's father, who could never say the *Our Father* without tears. Each month M. Martin took his turn in the nocturnal adoration of the Blessed Sacrament, while in their walks together in the country they loved to spend some time before the tabernacle in some quiet village church.

This home saw the birth of nine children, each from birth dedicated to the Blessed Virgin. After the birth of four girls they prayed much for a boy, one who should be a great saint and missionary; and one was given, only to be taken to Heaven after a brief four months on earth. They continued their prayers, and again a boy was born, but he, too, died, nine months after birth. Three more children followed, all girls, the last of whom was to fulfil all their prayers, nay to surpass them to an unbelievable degree. Looking at the calm strong face of the mother of St. Thérèse you realize how faithfully she fulfilled her duties as wife and mother, and how wisely and well she trained her children for God. For God was her first and last thought always.

Comparative wealth was not allowed to bring in its train the corrupting influence of luxury and indulgence, instead there reigned a patriarchal simplicity in which love never degenerated into weakness, and where the smallest fault never passed uncorrected. "Under what illusions the greater part of men live," writes this saintly mother; "if they possess riches, then they want honours, and when these are obtained they are still unhappy, for the heart which seeks contentment in aught save God can never be truly satisfied."

Look at her calm confidence in moments of sorrow after the death of four children: "Four of my children are already well placed, and the others, yes, the others, too, will go to the Heavenly kingdom more full of merit for having endured a longer combat. . . . When I closed the eyes of my dear little ones I experienced great grief, but it was a resigned grief. I did not regret having suffered for them. . . Life is short and full of suffering. I shall meet my dear ones again on high."

Then came the war of 1870-71, but before M. Martin's call to the colours could reach him it was over. Nine Prussian soldiers quartered in their house soon reduced it to a sad state of dirt and disorder. "Our home is reduced to a most pitiful state," she writes. "The whole city is in consternation. All weep except myself." It was in this year that M. Martin retired from business and took up his residence in the rue Saint-Blaise where two years later St. Thérèse was born on January 2, being baptized in the Church of Notre Dame two days later. But after a few months, Thérèse became so weakened that they feared for her life; in the midst of this anxiety came another, for Marie, the eldest girl, was sent home from the school at Le Mans suffering from typhoid fever. Day and night, undaunted by the double strain, the brave mother watched by the bedside of her child.

"Each one has her cross to carry," she wrote to Madame Guerin; "already you have to carry yours, and as you see life is not all roses. But God wills it in order to detach us from earth and draw our thoughts towards Heaven. . . . I never quit my child's side, and am on my feet day and night. It is really a special grace from God that I am able to keep up."

On May 5 she writes to Pauline: "This morning your father on his part made a pilgrimage in favour of Marie. He went and returned fasting, for he wished to add penance to his prayer."

Marie slowly returned to health and so likewise did little Thérèse, and when she was eleven months old her mother was able to write: "My little Thérèse walked alone on Tuesday. She is a sweet darling, like a little angel." The first thoughts of her children were directed to God. Thérèse was only two when her mother wrote: "She prays like a little angel. Every Sunday she goes to part of Vespers, and if unable to do so she is quite inconsolable."

But in this atmosphere of love faults were never passed over. When Marie was instructing the older girls Thérèse was not always invited. One day little Thérèse tried to enter the room, Marie watched her:

"She tried to open the door, but was too small to be able to reach the handle. I waited to see what she would do, whether she would call out for it to be opened. But no; she said nothing, in her helplessness she crouched down before the door. I told mother of this little adventure, and she said: 'You must not let her do that.' After a little while the same thing happened. Then I said: 'My little Thérèse, you are grieving little Jesus.' She looked at me very attentively and never attempted to do the like again." This is quite in accordance with St. Thérèse's account of herself at this age: "It was enough to say to me, 'You must not do that,' and I never wanted to do it again."

"All my life the Saviour has surrounded me with love," writes our little Saint. "My earliest recollections are of loving smiles and affectionate caresses. I cannot say how much I loved

121

Papa and Mamma; I found a thousand ways of manifesting it, for I was very open-hearted. My dear father's name fills me with happy memories. As soon as he returned home I always ran to meet him. Then he would walk with me in the house or garden, whichever I wished. Mother used to say laughingly that he did whatever I wanted. 'Why not?' he would answer, 'she is the Queen!' Then he would take me in his arms, place me on his shoulder and caress me. How happy I was then. Not only did I begin to enjoy life, but virtue itself charmed me. It seems to me that I had the same dispositions then that I have now. . . I had already formed the habit of not complaining when things were taken from me, and when accused unjustly I preferred to be silent rather than to excuse myself. . . How swiftly those sunny days of my childhood have passed away, how sweet the memories they have imprinted on my soul. I recall the happy days when Papa took me to the Pavillon (a little property belonging to the family on the outskirts of the town). Above all, I remember the Sunday walks when our dear mother always came with us. Even yet I feel the deep poetic impressions made upon my heart at the sight of the cornfields studded with cornflowers, poppies and daisies, in a word, all nature ravished me and lifted my heart to Heaven. Often during these long walks we met poor people, and little Thérèse was always chosen as alms-giver."

All too soon this happy family circle was invaded by the angel of death, who came to carry away the loving, devoted mother who was the centre of it all. After a long illness borne with heroic courage Madame Martin fell asleep in the Lord on August 28 of the year 1877 in her forty-sixth year. St. Thérèse was present at the administration of Extreme Unction, and years afterwards she writes: "The memory of this touching ceremony of Extreme Unction is imprinted on my soul. I can yet see the spot where I knelt and heard my poor father's sobs."

The shock of her mother's death made such a profound impression on St. Thérèse that for a space of ten years her naturally happy disposition deserted her. From being lively and demonstrative she became shy and timid, so sensitive that a look was often sufficient to bring tears, and she was only at ease amongst her dear ones at home. Speaking of this time St. Thérèse says: "Papa's affectionate heart seemed endowed with a mother's love, while you, Pauline and Marie, were no less tender and devoted."

They moved from Alençon to Lisieux soon after their mother's death and resumed family life, although it could never be the same any more. The two elder girls had charge of the house, and it became the scene of many joys and unforgettable family gatherings. Speaking of this time our little Mistress writes: "On awaking you (Pauline) were there to caress me, and I said my prayers beside you. My reading lessons followed later, and I remember the first word I could spell was *Heaven*. Lessons over, I hurried upstairs where Papa was usually to be found. . . . Each afternoon I went with him for a little walk, always paying a visit to the Blessed Sacrament in one or other of the churches in the city. That is how one day I saw for the first time the chapel of Carmel: 'Look, little Queen,' said my Papa. 'Behind that great grille holy religious are always praying to God.' I little thought that nine years later I should be one of them."

Our little Mistress tells us of the wonderful influence the Sundays and great feast days of the Church exercised over all the members of this saintly family: "The feasts! What precious memories those simple words recall! The feasts! How much I loved them! How well you (her sister Pauline) knew how to explain the mysteries hidden in each one of them. Yes, those days of earth were indeed days of Heaven. Above all, I loved the procession of the Blessed Sacrament. What a joy to strew flowers on the path of God! But before letting them fall I threw them up on high, and was never more happy than when some of my rose-petals touched the Sacred Monstrance. The feasts! The great ones were rare, but each week there was one very dear to my heart.

"Those joyous feasts which so quickly passed away also had their tinge of melancholy. My joy was unalloyed till Compline,[1] but after that evening office a sense of sadness pervaded my soul . . . and I longed for the rest of Heaven, the endless Sabbath of our true home.

"What shall I say of those united evenings at home? After a game of draughts, Marie or Pauline would read from the *Liturgical Year* or some other instructive book on the Faith. During this time I took my place on Papa's knee, and after the reading he would sing some melodious refrain to lull me to sleep. At length we went upstairs for night prayers; again my place was beside my father, and I had only to look at him to see how the saints pray. Then my little mother (Pauline) put me to bed, and I invariably asked: 'Have I been good today? Is God pleased with me? Will the angels be about me?' The answer was always 'Yes.' ... Then you and Marie embraced me and little Thérèse was left alone in the dark.

"I consider it a great grace that from childhood I was taught to overcome my fears. Occasionally you sent me to fetch something from a room at the other side of the house, wisely taking no refusal; but for this I should have become

---

[1] In most French churches Vespers are followed by Compline on Sunday afternoons.

very fearful, whereas now it is difficult to frighten me. I often wonder how you were able to bring me up with so much affection and yet not spoil me. You never passed over the least fault nor scolded me without cause, and you never went back on a decision once taken, as I knew full well."

There we have the picture of a true Catholic family life, simple, affectionate, loving, united, where the follies and vanities of the day found no place, and Catholics who wish to be the real thing cannot do better than model their own home life upon it. The only valid reason for entering the married state is because God wills it, and that in this state the soul will serve God better and give Him more glory because it is His choice. Here is a picture of married life given by Tertullian long ago:

"What is the union like of these two joined together in one hope, one discipline and one service? Both fellow-servants, not divided either in flesh or spirit. They are two in one flesh, and where there is one flesh there is one spirit. Together they pray, together make their resolutions, together they fast, mutually teaching, exhorting and supporting each other. In the Church they are together, at God's altar they are together; in trouble, in persecution, in consolation they are together. They hide nothing from each other and neither burden nor hinder each other. Together they visit the sick, give alms and aid to the needy; they make sacrifices without hesitation, and fulfil their daily work without hindrance . . . they sing the Lord's song together, and Christ beholding such rejoices. He gives them His peace, where these two are there is He, and where He is no harm can come!"

The first essential for the married state is that those who embrace it are truly in love with each other. This love must be mutual, for love alone will enable them to faithfully fulfil the duties of the state upon which they enter. A loveless marriage can only be a ghastly horror ending in a terrible catastrophe. Each one must be sure, quite sure that *it is love,* not some passing emotion, sudden passion or transitory fascination. What is true love? *True love is the constant unchanging direction of heart and will to one single person.* If they have this true love no matter what the sufferings and sorrows the future may hold, this love will carry them victoriously through all. If this love is absent all the wealth of the world cannot make up for it. No one should dream of entering the married state unless assured that their love is real and enduring and that it is returned in equal measure by the other. *It is not enough to love, one must also be loved in return,* and without this mutual love on the part of each no marriage can be a happy one.

This is all the more necessary seeing that marriage is not a matter of living together for a few years, but for life; once a marriage is validly contracted it can only be dissolved by death. When the Pharisees came to Jesus with their questionings about the married state He said to them: "What did Moses command you?" "Moses permitted to write a bill of divorce and to put her away." "For the hardness of your heart," replied the Saviour, "Moses gave you this precept. But from the beginning God made them male and female. For this cause a man shall leave father and mother and cleave to his wife. *And they shall be two in one flesh. Therefore now they are not two, but one. What God hath joined together let no man put asunder."*

Only the hand of God can separate, as says St. Paul: "A woman is bound by the law as long as her husband lives, but if her husband dies, she is free," and the same is true of the man.

It is because of its permanence that love, which alone can cement the union, is so essential. Then there is a second essential, unity of faith. How shall they dwell together except they be agreed? And how can they be agreed if divided on the most essential matter of all, the faith? What will be the effect on the children if the father goes one way and the mother another? "Be not unequally yoked together with the unbelievers" is as true in the twentieth century as it was in the first. True unity requires true faith as well as true love, for nothing unites and nothing divides so much as religion. *Between a Catholic and a non-Catholic there is a great void which cannot be bridged over.*

Besides this there must be assured means of subsistence for husband, wife and children. Sufficient means of subsistence, not great riches, for these are more often a curse than a blessing, but a sufficiency to provide a home in which the children may grow up reasonably cared for and educated in accordance with their state in life.

The union is *usque ad mortem* which *no state and no earthly power can sunder,* hence it is well on the first awakening of love that each should carefully consider the dispositions and character of the other. A person who is selfish, self-centred, arrogant, passionate, indifferent or irreligious before marriage will not become unselfish, self-sacrificing, humble, gentle, and devout by the mere act of marriage. It is vain to expect that one's influence after marriage will do what it has failed to do before. How great is the responsibility of those who embrace this state seeing they each hold in their hands the lifelong happiness or misery of the other!

Moreover, there is the tremendous responsibility of parenthood, the training of the children God may entrust to them in His love and love of country. How much may depend upon the future of a single child, what possibilities! He or she may become a great saint and do wonderful things for God and draw thousands to righteousness or become a devil and drag down a multitude to Hell.

Much will depend upon the training given in the first years, on the kind of atmosphere in which the child grows up! The home of little Thérèse shows the true ideal, the way in which from the moment when the child can distinguish yes from no he should be corrected. To wait till he is older is the strangest folly, for then ill-habits have been already formed and an after-remedy comes too late. Love and firmness, these two must go together, firmness must never degenerate into hardness nor love into weakness. If the child is wisely corrected during the first three or four years, wisely taught the things of God and the dawning understanding directed to Him, all will be well, and the work of guidance in later years will be easy.

Exact, instant and unquestioning obedience is fundamental in every Christian home, and neither tears nor pleadings of any sort must lead to a command being changed once it has been given.

A word must be said about vocation to the religious state or the priesthood. How often even good Catholic parents oppose, and oppose very resolutely, the very idea of any of their children dedicating their lives to God in this way.

How different was the attitude of the parents of St. Thérèse. One day her mother was reading the life of Madame Acarie, who, after having given all her daughters to Carmel, embraced the religious state herself. "What!" she exclaimed, "all her daughters Carmelites! Is it possible for a mother to have such an honour?" That was how the mother of Thérèse regarded religious vocation, and her father regarded it in the same light. When the last of his children (Celine) told him of her vocation to Carmel in a transport of joy he exclaimed:

"Come! let us pay a visit to the Blessed Sacrament together and thank God for all the graces He has bestowed upon our family, especially for the great honour He has done me in choosing His spouses from my household." While a religious vocation must never be forced, once it has been manifested it should not be opposed, but carefully watched in order to see whether it is a genuine vocation or only a passing fancy. If the signs of a true vocation show themselves, then the vocation should be encouraged.

There is one aspect of the married state which is often overlooked, and it is this: in embracing the married state those who enter it embark on a life of sacrifice and renunciation, not a whit less real than do those who embrace the life of the cloister. Many pleasures and much of former freedom must be sacrificed, for the care of the home and the training of the children demand it. This is where sacrifice comes in. Therefore, it is well to realize beforehand that *the married state involves a life of continual sacrifice* which will only end with death. This is why mutual love is so essential, for only love can give strength to persevere in sacrifice all day today, tomorrow, right on to the last day of all.

Sacrifice has always been characteristic of the married state, but never more so than now, because the Devil has introduced a system by which the pleasure of the married state may be enjoyed without the sacrifice, although sooner or later such a life brings its own punishment.

Fidelity to the law of God does press hardly on those who are faithful to it in these days, for next door to the Catholic family live a neo-pagan family, where no children come to prevent the continuous indulgence in pleasure of the two who live thus together. These go on after marriage just as they did before, there is no home life, they are always out at some place of amusement or another, nothing happens to hinder their pleasure until the coming of disease and death.

Now the Catholic father and mother have a family perhaps as numerous or more so than that of St. Thérèse. Their children have to be prepared for their future place in the world, they must be clothed, fed, educated—all this costs money; and the parents must continually sacrifice themselves for their offspring, deny themselves many innocent pleasures which they would enjoy. Is it any wonder sometimes that when they are feeling a little wearied with the struggle the Devil's crafty temptation comes upon them with overwhelming force: "What fools you are! Look at your neighbours, they have no children or only one, how easy and pleasant is their life compared to yours. See what I give to these who give themselves wholly to me. All the pleasures and delights of life, no ceaseless striving and struggling to make both ends meet, no continual sacrifices, no hardships, just a full life which satisfies all the demands of nature. The only child of your next-door neighbour, what a fine education he will have later on! And your children, they must have a very inferior education, they can never hope to hold the place in the world that this boy will have." How well the Devil argues and how real this neopagan world seems, and how far off the things of faith.

At such a moment the only answer is this: "I have embraced a life of sacrifice for myself and mine. I knew before I entered it that I must sacrifice and go on sacrificing till I die. I embraced this life because God called me to it and I will be true till death, be the price what it may. I have renounced the pleasures of the world willingly, knowingly, I have renounced them for my children, and if they cannot have the same position as the child of my neighbour they will have something infinitely greater, peace of heart which fidelity to the Law of

God alone can give. Yes, and I hear Him saying: 'I know where thou dwellest, even where Satan's seat is, but be thou faithful unto death and I will give thee a crown of life.'"

Only a few years ago I put the question: "Is England to follow France in the race for national suicide?"[2] Alas, already we have the answer. England has far outdistanced France or any other nation. This year the birth-rate in England is 15 per thousand to France's 18 per thousand. And I repeat now what I said then: "Neither nations nor individuals can defy the Divine Law and live. The nation which forgets God must perish."

---

[2] *The Real Thing,* pp. 125-6. Kegan Paul, Trench, Trübner & Co.

CHAPTER XIII
HUMILITY-TRUE AND FALSE

N the prayer said in the Divine Office and at Mass for the feast of our holy Patroness, we find these words: "Grant us, we beseech Thee, so to follow in the footsteps of the holy virgin Thérèse in *humility* and simplicity of heart, that we may attain eternal rewards."

What is humility? Alas, this most fundamental of virtues has been well nigh buried under the affectation and unreality of good people on the one hand and pious books on the other. In a single sentence St. Thérèse sweeps all these artificialities aside when she says, *"For me, humility is the truth."* Yes, true humility is to seek the exact truth as regards ourselves, and others.

Our Saviour valued this virtue so highly that in His only reference to His Sacred Heart He says: "Learn of me, for I am meek and humble of heart."

Never in the world's history has it been so necessary to insist on true humility as now, when the greatest evil in the world is pride. Pride of race, pride of achievement, pride of one's own powers and capacity, and overmastering sense of self-sufficiency which exclaims with Lucifer: "I shall be like unto God." Alas, pride is not limited to the children of this world, even amongst those of the Kingdom are to be found those who almost think their little efforts are necessary to support the Church, as if it were a merely human institution.

To the oncoming wave of pride God opposes the humility of the virgin of Lisieux. Humility is the truth. There is nothing exaggerated or extravagant about humility, it is just the bare truth about things, and our beloved Mistress, as she lay dying, reaffirmed her teaching: "Yes," she said, replying to Mother Gonzaga, "it seems to me that I have never sought anything but the truth. ... Yes, I have understood humility of heart!" Now, true humility teaches us first of all that of ourselves we are nothing, that all our gifts, whether natural or supernatural, have been given to us, hence we have no more reason to be proud of them than is the beggar who receives an alms: "If you have received, why glory as if you had not received?" Who called us forth from our original nothingness? Who has given us such power of intellect and will as we possess? God! He made us, and not we ourselves. Had I an intellect so great that it could penetrate all the mysteries of the universe, should this make me proud? What reason have I for pride, more than the poorest and most ignorant person in the world? Absolutely none.

God distributes His gifts as He wills, and if He has bestowed exceptional gifts of understanding on me they are His free gift and His alone. All my own efforts could not have added the most insignificant fraction to the power I possess.

If for an instant He withdrew His sustaining hand I should return to the nothingness whence His Almighty Word drew me forth. "He spake the word and I was made, He commanded and I was created."

And my intellect which likens me to God! Did He withdraw His hand I should be but a chattering idiot, unable to give expression to the simplest thought.

A proud person is a pitiful object, because nearly always destitute of those powers which he imagines himself to possess. The proud man is too proud to see that he is the laughing-stock of all who behold him. Pride is mental imbecility of the worst type.

What a light, then, does humility throw upon our natural powers, how completely it destroys the ground for pride in them, as though they had been acquired by our own efforts. The use of these powers is as dependent upon God for success as their first bestowal, for the exercise of the intellect depends upon His conserving energy, as its beginning depends upon His creating energy: "Except the Lord build the house, their labour is but lost who build it."

If pride in our natural gifts is so unutterably foolish, what shall be said of pride in our supernatural gifts? It is such self-evident folly that it seems incredible anyone should be carried away by it: "By the grace of God I am what I am," says St. Paul; that is the truth, and yet insidiously and in most unexpected ways pride creeps into the soul.

Every supernatural gift we possess is the free gift of God, a gift purchased for us at a great price, nothing less than the Blood of the Son of God. Of ourselves we can do nothing. Moment by moment we depend upon God's grace which works within us both to will and to do. We cannot perform the smallest supernatural action without it.

Our little Mistress realized this well enough, for in the August of 1897 she said to Mother Agnes (her sister Pauline): "If I was unfaithful, if I was to commit the smallest infidelity I should pay for it with such anguish that I should no longer be able to welcome death. So I never cease to say: 'My God, I beseech You to preserve me from the misfortune of being unfaithful'."

Of what unfaithfulness do you speak? "Of a thought of pride voluntarily entertained; this for example: I have acquired such and such a virtue, and I am sure I have the strength to practise it; for then I should be resting on my own strength, and when one does this there is danger of falling into the abyss. If I said: 'My God, You know I love You too much to dwell upon a single thought against Faith', I should have such violent temptations that I should certainly go under."

How well our little Patroness realized her own nothingness, how well she sees that the virtue of humility is the exact truth about herself, how she watched against even a passing thought of pride! On another occasion in reply to a sister who said, "You have always been faithful to grace?"; "Yes, from the age of three I have never refused God anything, but I must not glory in that. See this evening how the setting sun gilds the tree-tops; even so my soul appears shining and golden because exposed to the rays of love. But if the Divine Sun ceased to shine upon me, I should straightway appear shrouded in gloom."

We are everything and nothing. Everything with God's grace and nothing without it, for our Saviour has said: "Without me you can do nothing."

Never can we realize sufficiently our own utter helplessness on the one hand and God's sufficiency on the other. This is where the way of spiritual childhood comes in. Look at a little child who cannot walk, he flings himself into his mother's arms knowing that she is strong and will carry him. So it is with us; realizing our own helplessness we fling ourselves into the strong arms of God, knowing that He will carry us.

There is no pretence, no unreality in humility; humility is the truth. How often it is represented as something unreal and almost insincere, as when people pretend they do not possess gifts and qualities which they know perfectly well that they have. This is secret pride which expects praise from the hearer in return for self-depreciation. If we have gifts, whether natural or supernatural, humility requires us to sincerely admit the fact, while at the same time recognizing that they are gifts which we owe to God. A beggar cannot be proud of being given an alms, but he can rejoice at it, and so, too, we can rejoice in God's gifts and give thanks to Him for having bestowed them.

St. Thérèse well understood this, and writes: "If a little flower could speak, it seems to me it would tell quite simply what God had done for it without hiding its gifts. It would not say under pretext of humility that it was not pretty and was without perfume, that the sun had withered its beauty or the storm bruised its stem—if it knew such was not the case."

And she continues: "The flower now telling her story, rejoices in having to publish the wholly gratuitous favours of Jesus. She knows there was nothing in her capable of attracting His Divine glance; that it is His mercy alone which has filled her with good things."

And on another occasion: "To be little is not to attribute to oneself the virtues one practises, believing oneself to be capable of something, but to recognize that God puts treasures of virtue into the hands of His little child, to serve Him when there is need, but it is always the treasure of God."

Yes, the knowledge of the gift and graces we have received, far from making us proud rather increases the sense of our own nothingness.

The better we know ourselves the less we trust our own judgement and the more tolerant we become of the opinions of others; when the matter is an open question we never unduly press our own point of view and listen patiently to another whose opinion is not the one which appeals to us.

True humility makes us extremely merciful in our judgement of the actions of others; we only see the external act and not the motive which is hidden from us. Our little Mistress, speaking on this very point, says: "If the Devil brings before me the defects of a sister, I hasten to look for her virtues and good desires, saying to myself, if I have seen her fall once, she may have gained many victories over herself which she has concealed through humility, and the thing which appears to be a fault may be, owing to her good intention, really an act of virtue."

Humility teaches us to put the best and not the worst construction on the acts of others, and to always give them the benefit of the doubt.

The disciples of St. Thérèse promise: "To follow the way of spiritual childhood, taking up an attitude of *humility,* confidence, filial *abandon* and love towards God."

True humility, which is the truth, will never permit us to be rough and overbearing to others, for sweetness and gentleness are the natural fruit of a humble spirit.

CHAPTER XIV
THE PATH OF SIMPLICITY

OD is the Supreme Simplicity, therefore the higher the soul approaches God the more simple she becomes. Simplicity is not another name for stupidity as some are inclined to think, and as some spiritual books would seem to suggest; it implies absolute sincerity and singleness of aim and purpose: "If thine eye be single thy whole body shall be full of light." It means complete absence of all pretentiousness and unreality, and frank, open, sincere conduct in all the affairs of life. First of all, the soul has the most absolute singleness of aim, one purpose only in life to which all else is subordinated, to love Jesus to the fullest extent a creature can, since in loving Jesus all else is embraced. In the single act of loving Him we love all in Him, we desire all He desires, will all He wills and fulfil the whole purpose of our creation; since to know, love and serve Him down here and to be eternally one with Him in Heaven is the only reason for which we were brought into existence.

More and more as her soul progressed in love did our beloved little Mistress increase in this singleness of purpose: "Now I have no other desire, save to love Jesus unto folly! Yes, it is Love alone which draws me. I no longer desire either suffering or death, although both are very precious to me. . . . can no longer ask with eagerness for anything save the perfect accomplishment of the Will of God in my soul."

And speaking of those words of the Canticles, "'Draw me—we shall run'. 'No man,' says Jesus, 'can come to me except the Father who has sent me' — draw Him, and further on He teaches us that it is sufficient to knock that the door may be opened, and to humbly stretch forth the hand to receive. He adds that whatsoever we ask of the Father in His Name shall be given us. This is without doubt the reason that, long before the birth of Jesus, the Holy Spirit dictated this prophetic prayer: 'Draw me, we shall run.' In asking to be drawn, we seek for an intimate union with the object which has captivated our heart. If iron and fire were endowed with reason and the first should say 'Draw me,' would it not prove its wish of being identified with the fire to the point of sharing its substance? Well, such is precisely my prayer. I ask Jesus to draw me into the fire of His Love and to unite me so closely with Himself that He may live and act in me. I feel that the more the fire of love embraces my heart the more I shall cry, 'Draw me,' and the more also will those souls who come in contact with mine *run swiftly in the sweet odour of the Beloved.* Yes, they will run—we shall all run together, for souls that are on fire can never remain inactive."

Here we see that, as her soul became more single, love dominated all else, since she became more and more one with God, who *is* Love. Now this simplicity should gradually penetrate the whole of our life, no part of it should be withdrawn from its influence.

In this singleness of aim St. Thérèse of Lisieux and St. Francis of Assisi are remarkably alike. Love simplified the whole life of each one: "If we examine attentively the many saints that are in the Church, I do not know to whom you will compare the Little Flower if not to the Poor Man of Assisi or the Poverello if not to the Little Flower. Both of them brought

to holiness a nature that was strongly affectionate, a capacity
for love that was outstanding, and a temperament that was
artistic, sensitive to beauty under all its forms, not less
feminine in St. Francis than in the Saint of Lisieux."[3]
St. Thérèse attained perfection through love and not love
through perfection. Towards the end of her life she can say:
"My God, You know I have ever desired to love You alone. It
has been my sole ambition. Your love has gone before me even
from the days of my childhood. It has grown with my growth,
and now it is an abyss which I cannot fathom." By this burning
fire of love she was carried to perfection with the most
extraordinary swiftness, and her suffering and asceticism were
the fruit of love, not the cause of it. If her sufferings were
covered by a playful smile, they were none the less
tremendous, but love makes suffering a delight when endured
for the Loved, and this is why St. Thérèse speaks of her
sufferings as throwing rose-leaves to Jesus. "You ask me," she
says, "a way of perfection. I know only one—Love. I know
some directors advise counting our acts of virtue in order to
advance in perfection, but Jesus, who is my Director, does not
teach me to count my acts but to do everything for love." The
Little Flower, any more than St. Francis, would not have
accepted a mathematical piety.[4]

Both St. Francis and St. Thérèse were fascinated in their
earlier years by stories of Christian chivalry, the first by the
warrior-saints of Charlemagne, the latter especially by St. Joan
of Arc, and both desired to do as they had done, and both came
to see as our little Mistress has so well expressed it that: "The
only true glory is that which endures for ever; and to attain it

---

[3] *The Romanticism of Holiness,* by Father James, OFM.Cap., p. 139.

[4] *Ibid.,* p. 145.

there is no necessity to perform brilliant deeds, but rather to hide from the eyes of others and even from oneself."

St. Thérèse had another characteristic in common with St. Francis, a love of courtesy, for her sweet smile and gracious manner conquered the most obdurate, and she certainly made her own the thought of the Saint of Assisi: "Courtesy is one of the attributes of God, who sends His rain upon just and unjust. Courtesy is the sister of Charity, it extinguishes hatred and kindles love." Both, too, were singers, both sang their songs of love to Jesus in the same language; it may seem strange that St. Francis sang his songs in French, but so it was, perhaps because it was the language of chivalry. Listen to the fervent music of our little Mistress:

"I am Your Spouse, Your cherished Bride.
O come, Beloved, come, live in me,
Thy beauty ravishes my soul.
Deign to transform me,
Love, into Thee."

And these two had another characteristic, they were both artists, and had a wonderful love of natural beauty, for all created beauty lifted them up immediately to the contemplation of uncreated beauty; both admired the Divine Artist in His works.

Singleness of aim, then, must be the characteristic of the Disciples of St. Thérèse, like her we must be single, and like her come to perfection through love, since: "Love is more sanctifying and transforming than even the fire of Purgatory." Yes, in the single act of Love we embrace all else.

St. Thérèse chose the rose because it is the symbol of love and romance, and because she would emphasize the singleness of her aim—Love: "I will send down a rain of roses," she exclaims, her little sacrifices are rose-petals thrown to Jesus, and her many appearances after death have been very frequently accompanied by roses. Secondly, there is simplicity of life, the necessary consequence of singleness of aim, for as Love transforms the soul more and more into the Divine Image, she becomes more and more united to the Divine Simplicity.

Simplicity of life! As she advanced in life and God began to unveil to her the mission which she was to exercise in the world after her death, she realized ever more clearly that her life must be modelled on the Divine Simplicity, that there must be no extraordinary happenings in it because little souls could not follow her if this was to happen. When Mother Agnes said to her on the vigil of the Feast of Our Lady of Carmel, "Perhaps you will die tomorrow after Holy Communion!" she replied, "Oh, that does not resemble my little way in the least. To die of love after Holy Communion, that is too good for me: little souls could not imitate me in that."

She never desired visions of God or His saints in this world, because she would live by the light of Faith alone; what attracted her most in the life of the Holy Family was that it was all quite ordinary." She was attracted to St. John of the Cross because he was looked upon by some of his fellow-religious as rather less than ordinary. Visions, ecstasies, revelations, these things have no place in the "Little Way" which our holy Mistress set before us. She well knew the danger of these things, and how easily the soul may be deceived by false lights; she knew how safe and sure is the way of bare Faith alone, in which the soul walks securely without the danger of illusion or deception which extraordinary happenings bring with them. Loving God, the Blessed Virgin and the saints so very much, she never once wished to see them in this life: she was content to wait for the face-to-face Vision in Heaven.

Simplicity, too, in prayer. When she speaks to God she speaks with the affectionate loving confidence of a child to its mother. Prayer books are only a distraction for her, so she speaks to Jesus quite simply and unaffectedly, and tells Him all that is in her heart. We who run the way of love must imitate her, and we shall find a joy and delight in prayer unknown before. How many souls burden themselves with a multiplicity of prayers and practices which have little or no effect upon life, and often become a wearisome burden, prayers which they hasten to get through as quickly as may be. This is not the way of simplicity which our little Mistress would teach us. "Complicated methods of spirituality," she says, "are not for me." A loving glance at Jesus, and her heart is at ease at once.

Love is supremely simple, it looks at love and says, "I love you very much!" When love possesses the soul the sight of the Beloved is enough; love looks at love and is satisfied in the looking. The stronger love becomes the less the need of human words with which to express it. Then, too, extraordinary penances are not for the disciples of our little Saint any more than they were for her. She felt in the early days of her religious life, and even before that, an attraction to extraordinary penances, and it chanced that she fell ill from having worn a little iron cross too long, and remarks: "This would not have happened had not God wanted to make me understand that the macerations of the saints were not for me, nor for the little souls who wish to walk in *the way of spiritual childhood where nothing departs from the ordinary.*" Only a few weeks before her death she recommended moderation in penance "because more of nature than of grace often enters into them."

Our little Mistress found her sacrifices in the events ordained by Providence just as they happened to befall. Here is an instance. During her first year in Carmel she was given cider to drink in the Refectory instead of a home-made drink which was less strengthening. She happened to be placed next to a good old sister who shared the same exception and the same bottle of cider. This nun, afflicted by a malady which made her suffer much from thirst, did not perceive that she scarcely left any for her young neighbour, who, on her side, not daring to take water for fear of humiliating the sister, deprived herself almost entirely of drinking.

Here is another. When Second Portress, she was asked to prepare a lamp for which there was really no need, and she had a struggle to master her feelings about it. "To conquer myself I thought I was preparing a lamp for the Blessed Virgin and the Infant Jesus. Then I prepared it with the greatest care, not leaving a speck of dust upon it, and gradually I perceived in my soul a great stillness and sweetness. The bells for Matins sounded, I could not go promptly, but I had received such grace that if Sister had come and told me for example that I had made a mistake and must get another lamp ready, I should have obeyed her joyfully. From that day I made the resolution never to consider whether the things I was ordered to do were useful or not." These penances are far harder than self-chosen ones, however great, because in these nothing of self can enter. How often we find souls willing to make some great act of penance who will not try to give up some undesirable habit in which they indulge—fifty cigarettes a day and a steel discipline make a curious combination, yet they are not infrequently met with! No, true penance is hidden, and found in the ordinary circumstances of life, in bearing an unjust complaint patiently, in holding back a sharp retort when provoked, and keeping a smiling countenance even when verging on tears.

Simplicity again in reducing one's wants and necessities to

the minimum. How miserable most wealthy people are, surrounded by luxuries, their least fancy contented at once, and how angry if some trifling want cannot instantly be supplied. How unreasonable such people become, not to say unbearable! Never happy, possessing everything of earth, they possess nothing really worth having. The way of happiness is to reduce our wants to the very minimum. Do I really need this? *Is it really essential to life?* No, it is not! Well, then, there goes that bit of slavery, I shall not need it again. This means one want the less to supply, and so I am one point the happier than I was before. The happiness of life is not found in multiplicity, but in simplicity, for as the Saviour has told us, man's life consists not in the abundance of his possessions.

This is why St. Francis of Assisi and St. Thérèse were so happy, they had reduced their needs to almost nothing.

If you have only a few necessary wants, when one of these is wanting you can bear the sacrifice with a smile, instead of rousing the whole house by your complaints. Here, again, our beloved little Mistress shows us the way. One evening after Compline she looks in vain for her lamp, which another sister has carried off by mistake. This meant spending an hour in the dark just when she had counted on getting through a good deal of work. Instead of being annoyed she is happy in thinking that poverty consists in being deprived not only of desirable but also of necessary things.

What a joy it is when one day we discover that there is something we can really do without, which hitherto we had thought indispensable. What a new sense of freedom and liberty when we find we have one want the less. Yes, *happiness does not consist in the things we can do with, but in the things we can do without.*

Then there is simplicity in our pleasures and recreations;

the simpler they are the greater the pleasure they give. What recreation gives so much pleasure as a good walk in the country, the most simple, healthy and natural recreation of all. See the lovers of pleasure who spend their lives in its pursuit. They go to theatre after theatre, night after night, to dance after dance, and are simply bored to death by it all. Why is it? Because for recreation to give pleasure it must be something exceptional, a change from the ordinary round of life. When pleasure becomes a weary round of business it is pleasure no longer.

Again, simplicity in dress. The disciples of St. Thérèse will dress with great simplicity, without affectation on the one hand or extravagance on the other. When fashion offends against good taste and modesty they will *not* follow it. Simplicity of adornment, no ostentatious display of wealth, which is vulgarity at its worst! All beautiful things are simple both in nature and in art. The Church stresses the place simplicity holds in the life of our little Saint, since in the prayer at Mass it is joined with humility as the two principal virtues which she practised, and which we are invited to imitate.

Then, too, we must have simplicity when we happen to fall into one of those little faults or defects to which we are so often prone down here. Our little Mistress never wasted time in vain regrets: "When it so happens that I fall into some fault, I rise again *immediately*. One look to Jesus and the consciousness of my own misery atones for all."

CHAPTER XV
PRAYER-PUBLIC AND PRIVATE

H OW great is the power of prayer," exclaims our little Mistress. "Prayer is like a queen who always has free access to the King, and can obtain from him whatsoever she asks. It is not necessary in order to be heard to read some beautiful formula from a book composed for the circumstance—were this the case I should indeed deserve to be pitied. Apart from the Divine Office which, despite my unworthiness, it is my daily joy to recite, I have not the courage to search through books for beautiful prayers, they are so numerous that it would only give me a headache. . . . I say just what I wish to say to God and He always understands me." In these words St. Thérèse refers both to public and private prayer; to that intimate, familiar intercourse with God of each individual soul, and that solemn public adoration offered to God by those set apart for that purpose.

Prayer is one of the most marvellous gifts of God to man. To be able to speak to God and hear Him speaking to us in the interior silence of our soul on every occasion of joy or sorrow, in all the varied circumstances of life, this is a grace indeed.

For prayer under whatever form is a conversation with God, the soul speaking to Him and He speaking to the soul. One characteristic of prayer is its universality. We cannot all be priests, religious, learned professors, artists, but we can all pray, we can all in our own way make our hopes and fears, desires and aspirations known to God and hear Him speaking to us.

Listen again to our holy Patroness: "For me prayer is an uplifting of the heart, a simple glance towards Heaven, a cry of love and gratitude alike in moments of joy or sorrow. It is something high, supernatural, which expands the soul and unites her to God. Sometimes when I find myself in a state of great aridity and not a single good thought will come, I recite very slowly the Our Father or the Hail Mary which suffice to console me and provide divine food for my soul.' And not only does she speak to God, but she hears His Voice within her: I have never heard Him speak (that is, with the outward ear), but I know He is within me. At each instant He guides and inspires me, and just when needed new lights unseen before break in upon me."

Just for a moment we must consider these two kinds of prayer. First, the solemn public prayer of the Church offered by those consecrated to this work, solemnly set apart for it such as all those in sacred orders from subdeacon up to bishop, and monks and nuns whose rule binds them to the recitation of the Divine Office. When they thus pray they stand before God as the official representatives of His Church on earth. The Divine Office consists of the night and day offices. The night office is generally divided into three watches or nocturns, but on ferial days there is only one. The day office consists of Lauds said at daybreak; Prime, the first hour of the day, according to the Roman calculation of time; Terce, Sext and None recited at the third, sixth and ninth hour of the day; Vespers said as evening closes in; and finally Compline, which ends the round of praise and adoration. These hours are composed of psalms, antiphons, hymns, lessons and prayers, which vary according to the days of the week and the seasons.

During the course of the year we commemorate the whole life of the Saviour and the chief mysteries of our Faith, while sprinkled throughout the year, like stars in the firmament, are the feast days of God's Mother and His saints.

Many of God's children in all ages have loved to associate themselves with this prayer of the Church, and say either part or the whole of the Divine Office according to the time at their disposal.

Then there is the intimately personal intercourse with the Saviour in which the soul speaks freely and without restraint to Her Divine Lover; she may use words or she may use none. Generally she uses no set form of speech, and expresses herself in the way in which she is inspired at the moment. Now private prayer like this can be made to God anywhere, as we pass along the streets, while we toil at our work, while we travel in bus or train, no matter where we are or what we do we can always speak to God, sure that He on His part is always ready to hear us.

Again and again has Jesus insisted on the necessity of prayer and also given the assurance that we shall obtain all our asking: "Whatsoever you ask in My Name I will do." There are four conditions to be observed if our prayer is to be really efficacious.

First, *Attention.* Not merely the external attitude of the body, but the inward attention of the soul, for "God is a spirit, and they who adore Him must adore Him in spirit and in truth." To utter words without attention is to draw nigh to God with our lips while our heart is far from Him.

Second, *Humility.* For has not the Immaculate Mother sung: "He hath regarded the humility of His handmaiden," and is it not written: "God hath regard to the humble, but as for the proud, He beholds them afar off." The Pharisee in his pride was rejected, while the publican in his humility found acceptance with God. Humility is the truth, and we have ground enough for Humility once we know the truth about ourselves, our incapacity for all good, and our utter dependence upon God for everything natural and supernatural.

Third, *Confidence,* which springs naturally from humility, for while we see that of ourselves we can do nothing, we also see that through God we can do all things, so like our little Mistress, while we are filled with the most absolute distrust of ourselves, like her, we are bold to audacity in our confidence in God: "In Thee, O God, have I trusted; I shall never be confounded."

Fourth, *Perseverance.* To persevere in prayer proves we are in earnest; that is why our Saviour has insisted so much upon it. When the unexpected guest arrived in the night, the man in the parable goes to his friend, who will not rise and give to him, but he continues knocking and his importunity is rewarded. How often the prayer of years receives an unexpected answer; remember the persevering prayer of St. Monica, whose persistence gave to the Church one of her greatest Doctors. Indeed, the story of the Church is full of the most wonderful answers accorded to fervent persevering prayer. But, of course, all prayer is absolutely conditioned by God's will, whether expressed or not. "If this thing for which I ask is really for Your Glory, as it appears to me to be, then grant my request, but if it is not for Your Glory, refuse it, no matter what the refusal may cost me, for I would not ask for anything which is not absolutely according to Your Divine Will." I may not always express this thought, but it is always present, and the longer one lives the more one realizes that there is only one prayer which we can offer without any reserve, and that is that God's Holy Will may be perfectly done in us, and in all for whom we pray.

Prayer is vocal when we use words to express the aspirations of the soul. The public prayer of the Church, because it is for all, is always expressed in a set form of words, and our holy Patroness loved this public prayer so much, and desired to perform this work so perfectly, that, as she says, it was a daily martyrdom. How happy she was when it was her turn to recite aloud the prayers in the Divine Office and fulfil the duty of Officiant during the week! Prayer is mental when the soul prays without words, when, as St. Paul says: "The spirit prays within us, with groanings which cannot be uttered."

The power of prayer has no limits, since God has set none, and speaking especially of contemplative souls, St. Thérèse says: "While seeming to give nothing, they give more than Martha, who was troubled about many things. Jesus did not disapprove of Martha's labours, but of her over-great anxiety: for His Blessed Mother gave herself humbly to the same work when she prepared the repasts for the Holy Family. Archimedes said: 'Give me a lever and a fulcrum and I will lift the world.' What he could not attain, the saints have attained in full measure. For fulcrum the Almighty has given Himself, for lever prayer which kindles the fire of love; it is thus they have uplifted the world, it is thus that saints still militant have uplifted, and will continue to uplift it until the end of time." Again: "The Creator of the Universe awaits the prayer of one poor little soul to save a multitude of others, like her redeemed at the price of Blood. . . . Is not, then, the apostolate of prayer higher, so to say, than that of preaching?"

The Apostle tells us "to pray without ceasing." Now we cannot always be on our knees, but we can always pray, because we can make all the duties of the day our prayer. No matter what the task we can offer it up to God, so that our life becomes one long prayer.

About what shall we pray? About everything which interests us, for God is interested in all that concerns us, everything which affects us in any way; there is nothing which we may not speak about to Him. How wonderfully He shows His loving concern for us in all the ordinary affairs of our daily life, even the most insignificant! Nothing artificial or unreal should enter into our intercourse with God. We must speak simply, humbly, sincerely, without affectation or unreality. Jesus to His lovers is no far distant Divinity, but very nigh, dwelling with them, always at hand to help in every difficulty, to strengthen in every temptation, to console in every sorrow and rejoice with them in every joy.

The soul of the lover goes far beyond herself, for has she not at heart all the interests of her Divine Lover, are not all His interests hers also? Hence her prayer is apostolic, she would embrace all the souls in the world in the fervour of her zeal. Our little Mistress shows us how to direct our prayer: "I pray for all, without forgetting our priests at home, whose ministry is often as difficult as that of the missionary who preaches to the heathen. Like our Holy Mother St. Teresa, I wish to be a true daughter of the Church, and pray for all the intentions of the Vicar of Jesus Christ. That is the general aim of my life." Referring to her two missionaries she continues: "I unite myself in a special way to the two new brothers whom Jesus has given me. All I possess belongs to each one of them, for I feel God is too good, too generous to divide my offering. He is so rich that He gives without measure all I ask of Him, even though I do not spend myself in lengthy enumerations . . . the days would be too short to ask in detail for the needs of each, and I should fear to forget something. Complicated methods are not for simple souls, and as I am one of these, Our Lord Himself has inspired me with a very simple way of fulfilling my obligations.

"One day after Holy Communion He made me understand these words of the Canticles: 'Draw me! we shall run after you in the odour of your ointments.' O Jesus, it is not necessary to say in drawing me draw also the souls I love. These simple words, 'Draw me,' suffice! Yes, when a soul allows herself to be captivated by the odour of Your perfumes she cannot run alone; as a natural consequence of her attraction towards You, all the souls she loves are drawn in her train." There St. Thérèse shows us in all its simplicity the way in which to pray for others; our beloved little Saint says so truly in praying to be drawn ourselves we inevitably draw others with us: the closer we draw to Jesus, the closer shall we draw others to Him. In making the intentions of the Holy Father the special aim of our prayers we embrace the needs of the whole Church and the whole world, thus fulfilling the rule of the disciples of St. Thérèse by "imitating the apostolic spirit of St. Thérèse of the Child Jesus, praying for vocations and the sanctification of priests, religious and missionaries," because in praying for their sanctification we also pray for all the souls who will be saved by their ministry.

Then there are the saints of God, and with these friends in Heaven the soul, too, has converse, for they are God's friends who, in the glory of the Heavenly Country, are one with God Himself in a union which is eternal. Once they, like us, endured the conflicts of earth, they fought and struggled even as we; now they reign with Christ in glory, having overcome the world through the Blood of the Lamb and the word of their testimony. The saints are interested in all that interests us. How could it be otherwise? They hear our pleading! How? *In*

155

God. They grant our asking! How? *In* God. And not only so; sometimes, when it is God's pleasure, they come down to us upon earth.

The Blessed Virgin, God's Sweet Mother, is the greatest and most glorious of all the saints of God; she is so exalted in Heaven because her life was so humble and hidden on earth. Her life on earth was in all outward seeming quite ordinary, no ecstasies, no miracles, nothing to differentiate it from those among whom she lived. And yet she was God's masterpiece. But after her death? Ah, then she is exalted, miracles, wonders, apparitions of every kind in every land from the first wonders of the first ages down to the last miracles at Lourdes or in Rome: the story of the Church of God is the story of Mary.

And there is a likeness between the Immaculate Virgin and our little Saint, for she, too, was hidden upon earth, the great world unaware of her existence, a life quite ordinary, hidden as she had desired, even from those living beside her in the cloister. But afterwards? Afterwards her fame has gone to the end of the earth. Miracles have been multiplied to a marvellous extent, she has appeared again and again to those who have invoked her and she has verily fulfilled her promise: "I will come down."

In a quiet little country town of England a few years ago our little Mistress appeared to a quite ordinary little girl about ten years of age. The child was sick at the time and for three days the apparitions were continuous, and I can testify that the face of this child, usually so ordinary, was transfigured and lit up with unearthly light as she looked at the Saint. One morning St. Thérèse came and stood beside her, and placing her hand upon her head, said: "Father Benedict will bring you Holy Communion tomorrow and you will get quite well. I am going away and you will not see me again."

156

The child's parents had been much puzzled over these happenings, and when she told them what St. Thérèse had told her, they said to each other: "Now we shall just wait and see; this will prove if it is real or not." Late the same evening I thought: "I will just look over and see how the child is before retiring to rest." I talked with her and her parents with no thought in my mind of bringing her Holy Communion, but just as I was leaving, without reflection and hardly aware of what I was saying, I said: "You would like to receive Jesus tomorrow?" Then the parents told me what had happened. The next morning I gave the child Holy Communion. The apparitions ceased and she became as strong and well as before her illness and in two or three days was back at school.

I could relate many instances of her wonderful intervention at the front during the Great War of 1914-1918. One must suffice here. It was January of 1917 when we went up to take over the line in front of Marcoing, on the Somme. For some time I had hardly been able to see a yard in front of me at night after having been gassed up at Nieuport, and this night, when we detrained at Trescault to move up to the line, was so exceptionally dark that I had to feel for the mug of hot tea held out to me before the start; so the march along the road to Ribecourt and thence through the communication trenches to the front line promised to be a very perilous affair. That night was one of the most wonderful instances of the intervention of our Saint of which I have had experience.

Just before we fell in I said to her: "Sister, (she was not then canonized), if I am to come out of this alive, you will have to be my eyes to-night. You know I cannot see, so it is for you to help me." We moved off in the thick darkness for our hour's tramp to Ribecourt, and then a wonderful thing happened. A dull light seemed to shine from above my head, just like the sun through a London fog, which showed the road quite clearly for a hundred yards ahead. I saw our troops moving up and the relieved troops coming down, and the formation of the roadway, so I was able to avoid shell-holes when they occurred. I raised my head and looked up thinking the moon must be shining, but all was darkness, yet once my head was on the level the light shone down so that I saw everything quite clearly. After an hour's steady marching we passed through Ribecourt and entered the deep trench which zig-zagged up to Kaiser Trench. These were part of the old German defences of the Hindenburg Line and very deep. As we plunged into the trench I noticed the water was streaming down, the light still following me, the white flow was quite easily seen, sometimes it was so deep we had to mount the sides of the trench to get along. One thing I specially noted, when the very lights went up, instead of being in absolute darkness when they went out, I saw just as well as before. Even now as I write, so many years after the event, the memory of that night is still vividly before me and I seem to be treading the same way again, with the light shining above me. Finally we reached our dug-out, a very deep one, and made our way down the steep flight of steps and soon fell asleep in the heavy atmosphere which is characteristic of these underground shelters.

One fact is worth any amount of theory, and one great fact is this, that God and His saints do hear and intervene in this world of ours, as Catholics know full well. All God requires of a soul is sufficient sense and simplicity to realize that she is indeed the object of His special Providence, that He is concerned in all that concerns her, and will always give grace and strength for every need.

"Not a hair of your head," shall perish is God's sure promise, "Are not two sparrows sold for a farthing?" and is not the soul worth many sparrows, wherefore then shall she be afraid?

CHAPTER XVI
TWO-FOLD CHARACTER OF HER LITTLE DOCTRINE

HE spiritual life of St. Thérèse was based upon and drew all its inspirations from love. Her "Little Doctrine" takes this for granted: "I know of only one means by which to attain perfection: Love. . . . Love can supply for a long life. Jesus does not regard time because He is eternal. *He only regards love.*" ... "How sweet it is to love and be loved."

God made me to know, love and serve Him: without knowing there is no loving, for in order to be loved a person must first be known. And true, generous, self-sacrificing service can only be given by one who loves. So she sings in one of her last verses:

> "There is upon this earth
> A most marvellous tree
> Whose root is in Heaven.
> O wondrous mystery!
> And Love is the name of
> This wonderful tree."

St. Thérèse is a true artist, and with an artist's instinct she chooses as her favourite flower the rose, because it is the expression of love; her figure of the tree is also a true symbol since love has its origin in Heaven: God is Love and all love that is found upon earth has its origin from Him, whether natural or supernatural. Faith without love is fire without heat, and it is only when the soul loves that faith becomes a living reality. Why is it that so often in the modern world religion exercises little influence upon life; because it is divorced from love. The "Little Doctrine" of St. Thérèse has two characteristics; both the consequence of love. The first is the *active* principle, the desire to give pleasure to the Beloved; the second is the *passive* principle, complete *abandon* to the will of the Beloved. These two characteristics are found in all true love, whether natural or supernatural; they do not produce love, but love produces them.

Let us look first at the active principle as our little Mistress sets it forth for us in her "Little Doctrine" of supernatural life. This principle is a positive one, not the negative desire to avoid offending Jesus, but the positive desire of giving Him pleasure out of every action and duty of life. The negative desire may exist with little or no love, but the positive desire cannot exist without love, and the stronger the love the more intense becomes this all-consuming desire to please the Beloved. Not only is this way of seeking to give Jesus pleasure infinitely more consoling than the negative way of not offending Him, but in seeking to please the soul will surely escape offending Him.

Our little Saint from her earliest years began to tread this way, when a little girl of three she had already her little string of beads on which she counted her little acts of sacrifice and self-conquest, so thus, from the first, she trod the positive way so full of encouragement and consolation. Dear little Maria of Padua, her most intrepid disciple, did likewise, for she had her rosary of victories and at the close of day would say to Jesus:

"Look, Jesus, I have overcome myself so many times. I shall try to do better tomorrow."

Counting victories is more helpful than counting defeats, for so doing a soul advances more quickly along the path of perfection; the first inspires to fresh effort, the second only depresses.

The disciples of St. Thérèse take as one of their essential obligations that of doing everything for the pleasure of Jesus: "To watch with great purity and simplicity of intention in order to sanctify their smallest actions by Love; and not to lose a single occasion of giving pleasure to God."

Love transforms everything it touches, and the desire of pleasing the Beloved increases as love increases until finally the whole life becomes one act of giving pleasure to Jesus. Our work will be done with all the perfection and zeal of which we are capable, because Jesus has given us this work to do; the one through whom we receive our orders is merely the human instrument Jesus employs to convey His commands to us. Life becomes surprisingly different when we make this thought of doing all for Jesus our constant and inseparable companion. It helps in moments when we are exhausted and tired and feel we can do no more, when the day seems so long that it will never end: "Yes, Jesus," we say, "I can go on beyond my strength because it is all for You."

Our little Saint never gave in, even when her head was splitting she would go to the choir to recite the Divine Office because one foot could still follow the other. It is not what we are doing, but for whom we are doing it, that really matters.

This Positive way gives a joy and pleasure to life unknown before. All grumbling and complaining cease, and we become happy and light-hearted in the midst of the most fatiguing labour, remembering that we are the disciples of little Thérèse

163

pledged to live a life of joyous service of which she has given us such a wonderful example. She was always full of the joy of life, always made the best of things; never the worst. Joy is one of the most precious fruits of her Little Way, because it is a joy established on a foundation which is eternal.

A girl has a mistress who is never satisfied, do what she will; after doing her best and doing it well, there is no word of thanks, only a complaint that something or other was not done differently. What is she to do? She has done her work with a pure intention, to the best that is in her, because it is for Jesus. Well she knows He is pleased, and so she is not distressed because human appreciation is lacking. She can greet her mistress with a smile and feel no shadow of resentment because, like St. Thérèse, she looks through the natural and sees the supernatural.

This is not all attained in a moment. There will be falls, moments when dislike or anger will arise through a sense of the injustice of it all. Well, what is she to do then? The Rule for the disciples of our little Saint gives the answer: "Often renew during the day the interior disposition of fidelity; without being discouraged by falls or negligences which occur through weakness." Immediately an indignant feeling arises in the heart she must say: "Jesus, I am sorry. I will try to do better next time." We must never be surprised at our weakness, still less discouraged by it. "Look at little children," says St. Thérèse, "they are always breaking things, tearing their clothes or falling down, and all the while loving their parents so much." And speaking of these falls she remarks: "My God, I know I have deserved this feeling of sadness, but let me offer it to You all the same. I am sorry for what I have done, but I am glad to offer this suffering to You."

Again: "When I am tempted to be disquieted over some

silly thing I have said or done, I say to myself : 'Here I am at the first step again,' but I say so in great peace. It is sweet to realize how little and weak I am."

"Simplicity and purity of intention." That means having Jesus always in mind, remembering that it is He for whom we are working, never to look for human praise, but keep our eyes directed on Him alone. If our intention is pure and unmixed with any human motive we shall not mind if our best efforts are misunderstood. If, on the other hand, we work for those who are gentle and appreciative we must be the more on our guard to keep this purity and simplicity of intention; naturally a word of appreciation or sympathy is always welcome, but we must not rest on it, but keep our eyes fixed on Jesus.

As for our falls, Jesus knows all our weakness far better than we know it ourselves, and He allows for all to an extent infinitely greater than the most loving of parents. Above all, do not lose time in vain regret, because self-love is often mixed with this, a certain surprise that we have fallen. Children are not surprised at their falls, but get up at once and go on as if nothing had happened, and we who walk the way of spiritual childhood must do the same.

Again and again our little Mistress insists on this positive side of her "Little Doctrine." Only a few days before her death she said: "I have always remained little, having but one occupation, to gather the flowers of love and sacrifice and offer them to God for His pleasure," and: "I am only a very little soul, and work for His pleasure alone." Writing to one of her sisters: "If you wish to be a saint ... have but one single aim—to give pleasure to Jesus." And in another place: "I have no other means of proving my love than by scattering flowers; that is to say, to let no little sacrifice escape me, not a look, not a word, to make profit out of the smallest actions and do them for Love.

. . . Not one shall I see without shedding its petals before You."
And listen to her song:

> "To scatter flowers 'tis my first fruits to
> bring
> My faint drawn sighs, my long and
> anguished hours,
> My every pain, my joy, my suffering,
> These are my flowers."

This is the active and positive side of our Saint's little Doctrine.

The other is the *passive* side, the total, complete surrender of the will to the will of the Lover, to have no desire, no wish for anything, to renounce the power of choice that He may be the Chooser, to rejoice in His choice as it becomes manifest each day. This is the other side of her doctrine: *Abandon* absolute and complete in the arms of Infinite Love. This is the second characteristic, the surrender of the will of the Lover into the hands of the Loved.

This passive way of *abandon* is the fruit of love; only love can produce it, as only love can claim it. This complete *abandon* of all choice into the Hands of the Divine Lover is one of the most distinctive features of the "Little Doctrine" of our Saint, and she emphasizes it again and again. *Abandon* means much more than mere resignation. It means first of all that we say to Jesus: "Look, Jesus, I do not wish to have any free choice of my own in anything great or small. I want You to choose for me, and I shall be pleased with Your choice just as You reveal it to me, moment by moment, for in it I shall see my own." This is a renunciation which only love can make. It is the absolute trust and confidence of a child in its mother's arms, unconcerned as to where she carries it, and hence free from all anxiety.

Only a few days before her death, speaking to her sister, our little Mistress said: "Someone told me that I shall not have a death agony; all the same I am quite willing to have one."

"If you were free to choose to have one or not, which would you choose?" "I should choose nothing."

A little earlier in the same month in response to Mother Agnes's question: "Would you rather die than live?" she replied: "I do not prefer one rather than the other. What God prefers and chooses for me is that which pleases me most." On another occasion: "The only thing which pleases me is the will of God."

"Seek nothing and refuse nothing," that is the essential spirit of abandon. This is the delicious fruit of love as St. Thérèse has shown in those wonderful verses entitled *L'Abandon*, almost the last to come from her pen, in which she describes its wonderful effect upon the soul: "Sanctity," says our little Saint, "does not consist in this or that practice, but in a *disposition of heart* which makes us humble and little in the arms of God, conscious of our own weakness, but confident to audacity in the goodness of the Father." To seek nothing, wish for nothing save the perfect fulfilment of the Divine Will in herself and others, and in all the events and happenings in the world around her. To refuse nothing, to embrace everything just as it comes from the hands of God, whether it be joy or sorrow, sickness or health, success or failure. Once the soul comes to see that God's will is the sole reason of her existence, her whole outlook upon life is changed: she has become a new creature in Christ Jesus.

She no longer insists with vehemence upon any ideas of her own; instead, she says: "Jesus, this seems to me to be for the good of my soul, for the good of others or for the advancement of Your kingdom. If it is Your choice, then grant it, but if not, refuse it. I seek and desire nothing save Your adorable Will supreme over all." The soul exists not for herself, but for Him; completely abandoned to Him, she is assured that Jesus will do that which is best; and the best for her and those she loves is that she and they may become saints. Hence her prayer resolves itself into this: "Give to me and to all those I love and for whom I pray the grace to become saints, and do this in Your way because Your way is sure."

"Refuse nothing." Whatsoever Jesus asks the soul must give, cost what it may. "Refuse nothing." The physical suffering so exhausting and enervating, the terrible tiredness, the troubled nights, the mornings when we awake more tired than when we went to rest, when it seems as though if we move we must die, we must give this with joy, glad to have something to suffer for His sake who suffered so infinitely much for us.

Suffering is, or rather can be, a great aid to perfection, but it can never leave us quite as it found us. We are either better or worse, as Father Bernard Vaughan said in his characteristic way: "Suffering either drives us to God, or drives us from Him." Yes, everything depends upon how we act under it.

But for the soul who has become a disciple of St. Thérèse there is no question as to how she should act. She must accept the suffering joyfully and willingly. If her sufferings increase, so will her joy, for as our little Saint has said, if God increases the suffering He will increase the grace that we may be able to bear it.

But besides physical suffering, there is spiritual suffering. Days when everything is black without and within, when Jesus seems to hide Himself, and the soul is left alone with her own misery. Hard days, indeed, when prayer brings no consolation, and when even the coming of Jesus into the heart brings no relief. The soul in love with Jesus will be content, like St. Thérèse, to let Jesus sleep, and offer this desolating spiritual loneliness which is so hard to bear to His Divine Heart, not asking relief, but embracing lovingly this crucifixion of spirit which likens her more closely to Him.

So also will she act with regard to those whom she loves and who are joined to her by natural and supernatural ties. That Oza-like anxiety will not be hers. Poor Oza![5] How many like him feel the Ark of the Lord will not stand upright unless they stretch forth their feeble arm to sustain it. In moments when souls we love dearly are in danger how apt we are to imitate his impetuous act! How natural it is to feel that our presence, our words, our advice are so essential; very natural, but not very supernatural.

Often it happens that after all our efforts we have to leave a soul whom we have tried to help, feeling we have failed completely. St. Thérèse had experience of this, and speaking of an occasion when she left the parlour without having succeeded in consoling her sister Celine during their father's illness, she said: "At first, when she was in such grief, and I could not console her, I was heart-broken. But I soon realized that I was incapable of consoling a soul, and afterwards, when she went away uncomforted, I ceased to be distressed about it. I simply asked Jesus to supply for my helplessness. Since that time, when it has chanced that involuntarily I have pained someone, I ask God to pass after me, and torment myself no more."

This does not mean that we are not to do all we can to help and console a soul in need, but that we must do so without

---

[5]   2 Samuel 6:6.

anxiety, and follow the example of our little Mistress in asking Jesus to do that which we have failed to do, and then like her we shall find our prayer has obtained the relief we have been unable to give. "Be without anxiety," says St. Paul. We must do what we can, yet be undismayed if we fail to achieve our purpose.

Sometimes we see the work of a life-time overthrown in a moment; at such a time we need the spirit of *abandon* most. God says: "Yes! It is my pleasure that this work should be destroyed; you must make it yours also." That is only possible through Grace. Out of seeming disaster He brings a greater good, as we shall see in Heaven, if not down here.

Outward things can only trouble us to the extent that we permit them to do so; if we keep the window of the soul well guarded, then events without will trouble us as little as the scenes from a window out of which we are *not* looking. Our little Saint, speaking of this interior tranquillity, says: "If my soul had not been full of *abandon* to the Divine Will, I should have let myself be submerged beneath the feelings of joy and sorrow which succeed each other so quickly upon earth, and that would have caused bitter grief, but these alternations only touch the surface of my soul."

Things joyful and sad follow each other in such quick succession in this life that unless the soul remains in this state of complete *abandon* she will be carried away by the joy of one moment and crushed by the sorrow of another.

We must *abandon* ourselves as to the past, leave all to God's infinite mercy. A thousand different ways of acting on a particular occasion may present themselves afterwards, but we must not be disturbed. With the light we had at the time we have done what we have done. The past is past and nothing can change it, so we must leave it to God, praying Him to increase the good we have sought and undo the ill we have wrought.

We must face the future in the same spirit and not waste time in vain speculations as to what the future will bring for ourselves or for others. God holds the future, He is Infinite Love as well as Infinite Power and we know His Providence is guided by His Love. He sees all, knows all, sees the end of all, therefore we can trust Him utterly. Reflecting on the past or the future, regretting one thing, rejoicing over another, fearing another, are all vain and only unfit us to face the living present.

We must embrace this actual present in the same spirit of *abandon:* "This moment which escapes me and is gone," which is all we have in which to give Jesus the proof of our love; this present which, even as my word dies away, already speeds to eternity.

I choose everything and nothing. Everything because I choose everything God chooses for me; I choose nothing, because I have surrendered my choice entirely to Him. So doing we experience the truth of those other words of our little Saint: "God has always made me desire that which He willed to give me."

Our confidence is in God, not in ourselves, nor in creatures, and it arises from our passive *abandon* in His arms. The very knowledge of our weakness and frailty, the fact that we can do nothing of ourselves, assures us of God's help.

Our dear little Mistress says: "That which pleases God is for us to love our poverty and littleness, it is our blind confidence in His mercy which He loves." It may at first sight seem strange that our confidence should arise from the knowledge of our own weakness, and that as we grow in this self-knowledge, so do we grow in confidence, yet so it is, because confidence in God increases as confidence in self decreases.

As love grows, confidence grows with it until finally love casts out fear; for where fear is love is not perfected. Jesus desires our confidence above all things, nothing grieves Him so much as our want of it. Is not this true even of earthly love? What hurts so much as want of confidence? "I do not understand," exclaims our little Saint, "those who fear so tender a Friend."

In proportion as we come to know our nothingness there develops in our hearts a confidence without limits "in the Infinite Power and Goodness of God."

The soul must never lose confidence, no matter how great the conflict. We see how essential it is to keep our eyes fixed on Jesus in such moments from the example of St. Peter. When he saw Jesus walking upon the stormy waters he exclaimed: "Lord, if it is You, bid me come to You!" Jesus said: "Come!" and without a moment's reflection St. Peter is over the side of the ship into the raging sea to find the waters firm beneath his feet. But the moment he takes his eyes off his Lord, and looks at the waves, his confidence fails him and he begins to sink, but he has sufficient presence of mind to look again to Jesus and cry: "Lord, save me, or I perish." Instantly Jesus, stretching out His hand, lays hold of him, saying: "O thou of little faith, wherefore didst thou fear?"

God is almighty, and without His permission and within the limits fixed by Him no temptation can assail us. Our little Mistress was unafraid as she faced the last combat: "I have no fear of the last struggle, of sickness or suffering, however great it be. God has always helped me. He has supported me, led me by the hand from my earliest childhood. . . . I trust Him. Suffering may reach the extreme limit, but I am sure He will never forsake me." And a little later: "God gives me courage proportioned to my sufferings. . . . At the moment I feel I can endure no more, but I am unafraid; if my sufferings increase He will at the same time increase my patience."

If we realize the folly of trusting in ourselves, we also realize the folly of trusting in creatures who may fail us at the moment when we need their help the most. "How often," says the writer of the *Imitation of Christ*, "have I failed to find help there where I felt sure of it."

Our little Saint understood how little reliance we can place on human friendship. She first discovered this when only a little schoolgirl. Loyal, loving, affectionate, she had become very fond of two sisters who were pupils at the same school. One of them was absent for a time, and when she returned little Thérèse ran eagerly to greet her, only to be met with an icy stare, for the girl had quite forgotten she had ever known her. Thus she learnt the inconstancy of human friendship, yet with that wonderful loyalty so characteristic of her, she always continued to pray for this inconstant companion of her schooldays.

Yes, Jesus alone is our one unchanging Friend, whose Love is ever the same, and if we put our trust in Him we shall never be confounded.

CHAPTER XVII
RULE OF THE DISCIPLES OF ST. THÉRÈSE

IT was in the year 1929 that the Bishop of Bayeux and Lisieux erected in the Church of the Carmel of Lisieux three associations, the first for priests, the second for children, and the third for the adult faithful of both sexes. In constituting the association for adults the Bishop of Bayeux and Lisieux said: "We do not intend to complicate or multiply the various devotions to the young Saint of Carmel, but to achieve a unique work. In establishing the third section of a universal Association of souls desirous of advancing in Christian perfection under the protection and in imitation of the angelic little Saint of Lisieux we respond to the suggestions of the Sovereign Pontiff Pius XI who has said: 'All the faithful of Christ should study attentively in order to imitate it, the way of simplicity and spiritual childhood of St. Thérèse of the Child Jesus'."

Not a few Cardinals, Archbishops and Bishops, as well as some thousands of priests and many thousands of adults and children have been enrolled in this universal Association of our little Saint since its foundation in 1929. To all those, then, who are following the Sure Way of the young Virgin of Lisieux we extend our invitation to enter this Pious Union and so gain the strength that comes from unity.

All who love our Saint and attracted by her doctrine have taken her for Teacher and Guide, by entering this Association

175

will gain strength and encouragement and at the same time will take their part in realizing the wishes of the Supreme Pontiff, who looks for a great spiritual renewal of the whole world through the adoption of the Way of Spiritual Childhood.

Union with others gives encouragement in moments of difficulty, for we say to ourselves: "I belong to this Association of our little Saint, I am one of many thousands who endure the same struggles as I, what they are doing, I, too, by God's grace, can do. They are pressing on bravely along the path of spiritual childhood, I must be brave and courageous, too. I am one of little Thérèse's soldiers enlisted in her army, so I must bear a soldier's part in the fight, and like her, die: 'sword in hand'."

The little medal which I wear will be a constant reminder of my vocation, it will help me in moments of temptation, and enable me to rest with loving confidence in the arms of Jesus, and assure me that our little Mistress will not forget me in my time of need and will herself come to aid me.

The daily prayer will help to keep before me the vocation which I have embraced; that way "all love and confidence" which she followed with such fidelity and which now gives her such power with God.

Then, too, the various anniversaries of our little Saint as they come round will impress on us not only the various events in her life from birth till death, but will remind us of the particular aspects of her teaching which these days recall.

Moreover, we share in the prayers offered at the shrine of the Saint in the Carmel of Lisieux, the Mass offered there on the third Thursday of each month and the "Theresian hour," observed every Thursday from Easter till October for the intentions of the Associates.

Thus, by being enrolled in this Union of the Disciples of St. Thérèse we become more intimately united with each other and with our dear little Mistress through her home at Carmel where she spent the last years of her life.

Here then are the Statutes and Rule of the Disciples of St. Thérèse of the Child Jesus.

I. *End of the Union*

The Pious Union of the *Disciples* of St. Thérèse is canonically erected in the sanctuary of the Saint at Lisieux with the following aims:

1. To associate all who wish to place themselves under the special protection of the Little Saint of Carmel and intend to imitate her virtues by following *her Way of Spiritual Childhood.*

2. To promote in the Christian world a revival of the Evangelical spirit and Divine Love in opposition to the spirit of pride and independence which characterizes the present age, and is the cause of so much evil.

3. To respond with enthusiasm to the invitation of the Little Messenger of God and realize the desires of the Sovereign Pontiff Pius XI who foresees a salutary reform of human society through the universal practice of the Way of Spiritual Childhood.

II. *Rule of Life for the Associates*

The Associates, as a means towards these ends and to procure for themselves the more abundant protection of St. Thérèse and following the example and teaching of their Holy Patroness, will endeavour:

177

1. To follow the way of *Spiritual Childhood* by adopting towards God an attitude of humility, confidence, filial *abandon* and love which becomes a child towards the best of Fathers.

2. To watch over themselves with great purity and simplicity of intention in order to sanctify their smallest action by love; never to lose a single occasion of giving pleasure to God and to renew frequently during the day this interior disposition of fidelity, without, however, being discouraged by faults and negligences which may occur through weakness.

3. To approach the Holy Table as often as possible and to aim at daily Communion. The Associates are particularly invited to communicate the third Thursday of each month so as to better unite in spirit with the Mass offered for them that day in the church of the Carmel of Lisieux beside the tomb of their Holy Protectress.

4. To nourish a tender, constant and unlimited devotion to the Blessed Virgin, celebrating her Feasts with exemplary piety.

5. As true children of God and the Church to receive with filial docility and without discussion all the teaching and recommendations of the Sovereign Pontiff; for whom they will cherish a special veneration.

6. To be vigilant in the practice of fraternal charity in accordance with the evangelical counsels, so well understood, taught and practised by their Holy Patroness.

7. To preserve great purity of conduct so as never to offend the angelic glance of the Saint which rests upon them. Women and young girls enrolled in this Pious Union must strictly observe the laws of Christian modesty in their dress, in conformity with the repeated directions

of the Church and the instant commands of the Pope and bishops.

8. To imitate the apostolic spirit of St. Thérèse by praying for vocations, and the sanctification of priests, religious and missionaries and helping their ministry with charitable alms.

9. Finally, those who wish to follow the Saint more closely, may offer themselves as victims of God's Merciful Love by reciting the act of Oblation composed by her.

III. Conditions for Admission and Practices Recommended

1. The faithful of both sexes may be admitted to the Pious Union of Disciples of St. Thérèse provided they are over twelve years of age, and seriously resolved to observe the rule of life traced out for them and to perform the practices recommended to them.

2. The right of reception belongs to the Director of the Pious Union, appointed in accordance with Canon Law, or those to whom he delegates this power. The requests for admission must be transmitted to the Director-General with exact particulars of name, surname and address. Those who are admitted have their names inscribed in the special Register and receive as card of membership a picture of St. Thérèse of the Child Jesus.

3. These Associates of this Pious Union are obliged (but not under pain of sin even venial):

(a) Always to carry respectfully on their person a blessed medal of their Holy Patroness. It will be given to them at Lisieux if they can go there; those who cannot will receive it from a priest authorized by the Director of the Pious Union.

(b) To recite privately each day the following prayer which is said in the Church of Carmel of Lisieux every evening at Benediction of the Blessed Sacrament:

"O Heavenly Father, who through St. Thérèse of the Child Jesus would recall the world to the Merciful Love which fills Your Heart, and the filial confidence we should have in You, we humbly thank You for having bestowed so much glory on this Your ever faithful child, and for having given her such a marvellous power of daily drawing to You a great number of souls who will praise You eternally.

"Holy "Little Thérèse," be mindful of your promise of doing good upon earth, send down an abundant rain of roses upon those who call upon you, and obtain for us from God the graces we look for from His Infinite Goodness.

"St. Thérèse of the Child Jesus, draw us along your *little way* of love and confidence that so you may lead us to God Our Father in Heaven. Amen."

(c) To keep with special fervour and if possible receive Holy Communion on the principal anniversaries of Saint Thérèse and especially on the Liturgical feast of October 3. These anniversaries are the following:

Birthday, January 2; Baptism, January 4; Smile of the Blessed Virgin, May 13; First Communion, May 8; Confirmation, June 14; Grace of Christmas, December 25; Entrance into Carmel, April 9; Reception of habit, January 10; Profession, September 8; Taking of the Veil, September 24; Oblation to Divine Love, June 9; her precious death, September 30; Beatification, April 29; Canonization, May 17.

IV. *Spiritual Advantages and Official Organ*

1. The members of the Pious Union participate in the indulgences, privileges and other graces conceded or hereafter to be conceded to this Union, in the daily prayers said in the Sanctuary of the Saint by the Carmelite nuns of Lisieux and the pilgrims. The prayer referred to above is recited for them every evening; Mass is offered the third Thursday of every month, and the same day the Theresian hour is offered for their intentions from Easter to the first of October.

The Official Organ of this Union is the Monthly Review: *Les Annales de St. Thérèse de Lisieux.*

The following is the act of Oblation referred to above, composed by St. Thérèse herself:

"In order to live in an act of perfect love, *I offer myself as a victim of Holocaust* to Your Merciful Love, beseeching You to consume me unceasingly, and to let the floods of Infinite tenderness which are pent up within You to overflow into my soul that so, O God, I may become a martyr of Your Love.

"May this martyrdom, after having prepared me to appear before You, free me from the body, that so my soul may fly without delay into the eternal embrace of Your Merciful Love.

"I wish, O my Beloved, at each beating of my heart to renew this offering an infinite number of times 'till the shadows flee away,' and I can tell You my love face to face everlastingly."

To this offering is attached a partial indulgence of three hundred days each time it is recited; a plenary indulgence once a month on the usual conditions to those who recite it every day.

By a rescript of June 20, 1932, the Pious Union at Lisieux was raised to the dignity of a union *Primaria* and by a rescript of August 1 the following indulgences were accorded:

ST. Thérèse and the Faithful

1. A plenary indulgence on the day of admission to the Pious Union.

2. A plenary indulgence on the anniversary of the death of St. Thérèse (September 30) to all members.

3. A partial indulgence of seven years to the Disciples of the Pious Union who take part in the Retreats given at Lisieux.

4. A partial indulgence of one hundred days to the Disciples of the Pious Union each time they say the Pater, Ave and Gloria, together with the following prayer: "St. Thérèse of the Child Jesus, draw us along your *little way* of love and confidence that so you may lead us to God Our Father in Heaven." Amen.

CHAPTER XVIII
THE BASILICA OF LISIEUX

❧

T was only in 1926 that the erection of the great Basilica was decided upon owing to the increase in the number of pilgrims who were coming to Lisieux, not only from France, but from every part of the world. When the Church at Carmel was enlarged by an extension of the nave in view of the Beatification in 1923, it was thought that the additional space would more than provide for the needs of the pilgrims. But already in the course of 1925, the year of canonization, the number of Masses said in the Carmelite Church numbered over six thousand and by 1930 they had increased to nearly ten thousand.

The site chosen was on the hill outside the city overlooking the station, and here the foundation stone of this vast structure was laid on September 30, 1929. Two years later, on the anniversary of the Canonization, May 17, the immense terrace in front of the future Basilica, capable of accommodating hundreds of thousands, was solemnly inaugurated. On July 3, in 1932, the lower church of the Basilica was blessed by Mgr. Maglione, Apostolic Nuncio from the Holy See to France, in the presence of a vast multitude of the faithful.

On Easter Monday of 1934, the last day of the Holy Year, commemorating the nineteenth centenary of Redemption, the magnificent Way of the Cross and the great Calvary behind the Basilica was inaugurated by Cardinal Liénart.

It is the hope of all clients of St. Thérèse that the year 1937, the fortieth anniversary of her going to God, may see the consecration of the great upper Church which is now in course of erection.

I must admit that when first I heard of this project I felt considerable misgivings as to the possible result, because so many modern shrines are far from being either beautiful or artistically satisfying.

But in truth I should not have been so fearful for is not our little Saint an artist, and would she not, therefore, exercise her powers and see to it that the great sanctuary, which was destined to arise on the heights outside her own city, should be not only a great centre of prayer and devotion, but also a monument of real beauty, which should mark a new era in the artistic as well as in the spiritual world? And such it is, for surely our little Saint herself must have inspired the architect and artists associated with him in the realization of this remarkable work!

After a long artistic sleep, in which the copying of ancient examples has been universal throughout Europe, there are signs of the awakening of new life, and we are witnessing the birth of a new style of architecture, which we hope will not be unworthy to compare with the glorious achievements of former times.

The Basilica of Lisieux holds the front rank in this new movement, and what has been already realized gives the assurance that when complete this great Sanctuary will be the most outstanding artistic achievement of our century. The vast terrace, a great level space with its retaining wall of grey granite and austerely simple balustrade with fourteen pylons, also of granite, surmounted by the strikingly original bronze lanterns, produces a remarkable impression of spaciousness and grandeur as one comes upon it after ascending the hill from Lisieux.

From this spot a magnificent view of the city of Liseux below and the surrounding hills can be obtained. On the opposite side, reaching the whole length of the terrace, stands the lower story of the cloisters, which stretch out on either side from the great flight of steps leading up to the entrance of the future upper church. At the top of this flight of steps a temporary sanctuary has been formed at which, when there is an exceptionally large influx of pilgrims, Mass is celebrated.

The choice of grey granite as the external material for the Basilica is an admirable one; its texture weathers well in this atmosphere, and it also demands a simplicity of treatment which assures the monumental character of the building. The design of the lower portion of the cloisters is marked by great simplicity. The windows are segment-headed with a deep moulding and the same treatment is followed for the two entrance arches, with their very original wrought iron gates, leading down to the lower church. When the open arcade is added we shall see the value of this solid mass of granite walling below. A flight of steps on either side lead down to the lower church, which is as beautiful as it is original.

The plan of this lower church consists of a wide nave of five bays with aisles nearly as wide, and three arched chapels on either side, each containing two altars. The great narthex consists of two bays of unequal length. The vaults are supported on cylindrical columns of cream-coloured marble, with square white marble capitals, carved in low relief with very simple floral ornament, dividing the nave from the aisles.

The walls are faced with cream-coloured marble up to the height of the capitals, terminated by a narrow sunk frieze of conventional ornament with the ground slightly gilt, just

185

sufficient to throw the ornament into relief. The walls and vaulting above this level are covered with mosaic, and it is here that the originality and beauty of the design become most accentuated. In the place of the usual gold background a new treatment has been followed, the ground is of a varied cream white sprinkled with gold, so that while there is a shimmer of gold everywhere, it is never so much as to be oppressive; moreover a small amount of silver is mingled with the gold.

The rich coloured ornament is concentrated on the springing of the vaulting from the capitals, which gradually dies away as the vault rises and then the lines of the arches are carried across in richly decorative bands, in which blues predominate. Roses of conventional character form a great part of the decorative detail.

The marble balustrade of the communion rail separates the nave from the sanctuary. The high altar is of bronze gilt, as is also the tabernacle, cross, and candlesticks, all ornamented with very simple, but effective detail.

Above the altar stands the magnificent figure of St. Thérèse in white marble, the work of the Trappist monk, Dom Marie-Bernard, remarkably architectonic with arms upraised in prayer, a triumph of the sculptor's art.

But how can this sculptured figure be harmonized with the great mosaic background? Well, it has been done so successfully that you do not even notice the contrast between the two materials. Behind the statue and forming, so to say, a background to it, is a cross of very broad proportions, against which the white figure stands out, while above the head are roses which give the impression that she has just thrown them up. Then, on either side of the cross, are the figures of angels bearing baskets of roses.

Those nearest the cross are kneeling, the second pair are

186

inclining and the third standing; thus the composition rises towards the sides as it ought.

The drapery is admirably drawn and the faces of the angels are really beautiful, a rarity in modern mosaic, where, as a rule, the design is crude and unfinished. The whole treatment of the Sanctuary is as harmonious as it is beautiful and satisfying.

On the Epistle side is the Altar of Our Lady, who is represented by a gilt figure reproducing the Madonna of the apparition. The east wall is covered with mosaic ornament in which roses predominate. On the Gospel side is the altar of the Child Jesus, and here beneath a canopy is a gilt figure of the Child Jesus, reproducing one of which St. Thérèse was very fond. Every detail of the Sanctuary down to the very smallest, displays a most remarkable combination of originality and a homogeneous beauty that is very satisfying.

With the exception of the altar-piece behind the high altar there is no other figured work in the whole Basilica, but there are vacant spaces for the stations of the Cross and certain other work which will be completed later on.

The oak benches, very simple and solid, like all else, have been specially designed.

In the side chapels the altars are each of different design, but the general lines are the same, the difference is in the detail. Here, too, everything is in harmony, even the candlesticks and cross being specially designed. These altars are supplied with four candlesticks instead of six, which is the Roman custom, and I think their appearance would be improved if the two additional candlesticks were added.

The electric light fittings, too, are an interesting and original feature, placed high up in the vault so that the light comes wholly from above, as it ought. The carved oak confessionals along the west wall of the narthex are excellent examples of the woodcarver's art.

But it is the unity of the whole, the perfection and harmony of colour, materials, ornament, down to the smallest detail, which impress so much. Such a unity as I have not seen elsewhere in any modern work. The colour harmony must be seen and studied under the varied light of different times of day to be fully appreciated.

I am pleased to see that as he develops his work the architect is always moving towards a greater simplicity, and it is this trend which gives assurance that the vast upper church will at least equal in unity and perfection this lower church, which is such a triumph of creative art.

Has it any prototypes? Well, the only work in recent times at all comparable to it is the lower church at Monte Cassino, the work of the Beuron Benedictines. Of course, Monte Cassino is on a much smaller scale than that of Lisieux, but as I remarked, at the time of its completion, it showed great originality and beauty, and the high altar with the two figures of SS. Benedict and Scholastica sitting in the rainbow is something not easily forgotten. Neither has the work at Monte Cassino attained quite the same unity as has the work at Lisieux, though in many ways it may be looked upon as its precursor.

Perhaps the lower church of Assisi approaches most nearly to that of Lisieux, both in extent and general effect, than any other work of which I have cognizance, with this difference, however, that Assisi is covered with frescoes, while Lisieux is covered with mosaics, for frescoes would not resist well in the humid atmosphere of Normandy.

Lisieux shows the real test of genius because it satisfies alike the technical expert and the artist on the one hand and the humblest worshipper on the other. Both alike feel the fascination of its wonderful unity and artistic beauty, although each would express themselves in different language concerning it.

How has it been possible in this time of universal distress to find the means for this great work? The whole world has united in offering its tribute to the Saint of Lisieux, above all, France and Belgium, who have given in most generous measure. And who are the contributors? Mostly the poor and the humble. There have been very few large offerings. . . . It is by means of small gifts of a few francs apiece that this wonderful shrine is rising, each gift made at the cost of no little sacrifice. And the remarkable thing about it is this, each week there flows in just enough to meet the need, there is never any great reserve in hand; just sufficient for the demands of the moment. Perhaps, with Norman prudence, our little Patroness sees that this is best, for with the variations in values which are constantly occurring a great sum might easily become a small one, so she provides, according to her own teaching, "for a day at a time."

I hope many of my readers may be able to go and see this wonderful work which is being realized at Lisieux, for it is easily accessible, at least, from the British Isles.

Many of St. Thérèse's humble followers have, I know, desired to have their part in the raising of this sanctuary, but have been deterred through fear as to the complications involved in sending small offerings abroad; well, for their consolation I may say all they need do is to get just an ordinary British Postal Order for the sum they wish to send, make it payable to the *Carmel of Lisieux* and address the letter to Rev. Mother Superior, Carmel de Lisieux, Lisieux, Calvados, France.

Surely it is not without a special providence that the Basilica should be building in this time of distress, for it

189

provides assured work for a great number who would otherwise be workless. What a blessing it has been to many a poor artist! Thus this sanctuary which is rising as a loving act of homage to God is also an act of charity to the neighbour, and gives another instance of the fact that love of God and love of the neighbour go hand in hand as our little Mistress has so constantly insisted.

The Basilica of Lisieux

CHAPTER XIX
THE PILGRIMAGE OF LISIEUX

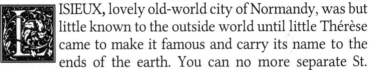

ISIEUX, lovely old-world city of Normandy, was but little known to the outside world until little Thérèse came to make it famous and carry its name to the ends of the earth. You can no more separate St. Thérèse from Lisieux than you can St. Francis from Assisi, these two saints and their cities are bound together in irrevocable unity.

Situated amidst the wooded hills of the beautiful Norman country, Lisieux is, as regards size, a comparatively small city of some 16,000 inhabitants, but with its very fine Gothic churches and quaint medieval houses has always had an attraction for artists.

Quite naturally, all the lovers of little Thérèse long to visit this place, associated as it is with the greater part of her life and with her glorious death.

It is easy for inhabitants of the British Isles to make a pilgrimage to the city of St. Thérèse. The most direct and inexpensive route is by boat from Southampton to Havre. The boat leaves in the evening and reaches Havre the following morning. You have then to take a small steamer across the Seine to Honfleur on the opposite side, and thence the train takes you to Lisieux in the short space of an hour.

Those who do not like quite such a long sea passage can cross the Channel from Newhaven to Dieppe, and thence, via Rouen, to Lisieux. Those who come from Paris will take the train from the Station of St. Lazare, whence the train runs direct to Lisieux, the journey taking a little over three hours.

On leaving the station at Lisieux, on the side of the hill to your right you will notice the great granite retaining wall of the terrace in front of the Basilica, with its pylons surmounted with lanterns, which give the impression of being a series of lighthouses, which, in one sense, indeed they are. Above the balustrade you will see the scaffolding of the upper church of the Basilica.

To reach the Carmel of Lisieux, naturally the first object of the pilgrim's visit, on coming out of the station you go straight on along the rue de la Gare, and the second turning on your right is the rue du Carmel, formerly the rue de Livarot. A short way along this street, on the right, is the Carmel of Lisieux, within which our little Mistress spent the last nine years of her life. The church will be recognized at once, for postcards and photographs have made it famous the world over.

The front has been brought nearer the road than it was in the time of St. Thérèse, as the church was enlarged in 1923 in view of the increasing number of pilgrims coming to Lisieux. At that time the additional space was thought amply sufficient as the extraordinary development of the pilgrimage since, which necessitated the creation of the Basilica on the hill outside the city, was not foreseen.

The church is Renaissance in style, dating from the seventeenth century, when both church and convent were erected. Internally, the appearance of the church is very much what it always was, for the authorities wisely decided to conserve as far as possible its original aspect and to harmonize the new work with the old.

On the Gospel side a narrow aisle has been added in which there are a series of chapels, and the high altar is new, a good example of the Renaissance style which, in its general proportions, preserves the lines of the original altar, which was of oak and may be seen in the sacristy.

On the Epistle side of the nave, about half-way up from the entrance, is the large semicircular chapel which forms the shrine of our Saint. The opening from the nave is closed by a very fine wrought iron screen. Two altars on either side of the opening, both the gift of Father Taylor of Carfin, enable Mass to be said at the shrine by two priests at the same time. The walls about these altars are covered with innumerable military decorations, the offerings of the soldier-clients of our little Saint.

Within the great iron screen, on the chord of the apse, stands the tomb of St. Thérèse. The base is composed of variously coloured marbles, simply, but excellently designed, and above is the figure of the Saint, lying in the position in which she died, with face turned towards the spectator. The upper portion of the shrine, in which the figure of the Saint reposes, is enclosed in a finely ornamented bronze gilt framework which forms a canopy over the Saint. The allegorical group of angels and the child (who symbolizes St. Thérèse) have been thought by some to detract from the central figure, but when the marble is mellowed by age the effect will be more satisfying. Of course, the figures are in Renaissance style, to which the artist was bound by the necessity of the case.

There is a fine marble pavement to the chapel, and under a canopy high up on the wall behind the shrine is the famous "Virgin of the Smile" which came miraculously to life on the occasion when St. Thérèse was healed of her dangerous illness.

In an opening above the high altar is a very fine allegorical group. Beneath the cross the Blessed Virgin is seated with the

Child Jesus on her lap. Kneeling before her is St. Thérèse, who, taking the roses which the Mother and Child hold for her, is casting them upon the earth. From the arms of the cross depends the cloth of Veronica showing the Holy Face. This group is admirable, both in design and execution, and worthy of special notice.

On the right of the sanctuary, the Epistle side, is the great grille of the nuns' choir, and beyond it the Communion grate. As one listens to the voices of the nuns reciting the Divine Office one remembers that the voices of three Carmelite sisters of St. Thérèse are mingled with them, and the thought brings the Saint very near. Yes, behind that grille for nine years St. Thérèse had her part in that solemn round of prayer and praise, there at the Communion grate she received the Jesus she loved with such passionate ardour. On the Gospel side, near the the inner sacristy, is the entrance to the Convent, and through this door St. Thérèse and her sisters all passed in turn when they came to give themselves to Jesus in the cloistral life. In the sacristy, which is on the left as you enter, you are shown the precious relics of our Saint, her religious dress and many other interesting souvenirs.

Here in this holy place prayer rises the day long from the stream of pilgrims who come from afar to pray in the very church in which our beloved little Patroness sang the praises of the Saviour. And the quiet, serious bearing of the pilgrims impresses you at once; they are not mere sight-seers, they are all in deadly earnest, they have come in a spirit of recollection to pray and worship in union with our little Saint. While I was saying Mass at the shrine the church would empty and refill, yet so wonderfully quiet were the pilgrims in their movements in and out that I was scarcely aware of it.

Then, too, the modest dress and behaviour of the pilgrims

194

impresses very much. The whole atmosphere is one of prayer and recollection.

After having seen the Convent-home of St. Thérèse, the pilgrim's next thought will be to see Les Buissonnets, her home until she entered Carmel.

Turn to the right on leaving the church and after passing the fine Gothic church of St. Jacques (also on your right), continue your way until you enter the Boulevard Herbert Fournet, and on your right you will see a large new hotel, then passing up the narrow street alongside this and turning first to the left and then to the right, a few steps further on your left is the entrance to Les Buissonnets. You enter and are surprised at the extent of the garden which, enclosed on all sides, seems to be shut off from the outer world very completely. A wonderful sense of peace reigns over it. The house is familiar to all, for those who have not seen some representation of it are very few. Outwardly it is just as it was when St. Thérèse, with her father and sisters, lived in it, and at every turn we are reminded of the many incidents of her early life. In that room to your left as you face the house little Thérèse had the vision of the Blessed Virgin when in an instant she was miraculously cured. It was to that window Léonie carried her after she had failed to recognize her sister Marie, and it was down here in the garden that poor Marie, with outstretched hands and upturned face uttered her pitiful cry of "My little Thérèse" in a vain effort to win back recognition to the mind of her sister, to whom, a few moments later, the Blessed Virgin herself brought perfect healing.

As you enter the hall you notice the fireplace where our little Saint placed her shoes to receive the expected gifts of Christmas night. Beyond is the room in which the family spent their evenings together of which our little Saint has left such charming records. Nothing has been changed, even the furniture remains as it was on that last unforgettable night before she entered Carmel. That last family gathering took place on the evening of April 8, in the year 1888.

On the first floor is M. Martin's bedroom; here, too, all remains just as when he occupied it. The room of St. Thérèse has been slightly changed. The alcove in which her bed had place is now occupied by an altar. The statue of the Blessed Virgin is an exact copy of the original which, as we have mentioned, is now in the shrine at Carmel, and occupies the same place as at the time of the apparition. A tiny sacristy at the side just allows space for the priest to rest. By chance I was in Lisieux on the anniversary of the apparition and said Mass at the altar in what is certainly one of the most sacred places in Lisieux. I set off very early in the morning in company with the Vicar-General of an Indian diocese, and we served each other's Mass in turn. The memory of that beautiful May morning in the silence of this upper room will long remain in our memory.

In another room may be seen the bed of St. Thérèse, her toys and school-books and other souvenirs of her early years.

You pass from the house into the spacious garden. Here, facing the house, on the very spot on which it took place, is a marble group showing St. Thérèse with her father on that memorable Whit-Sunday afternoon when she made known to him her vocation. The figures are very admirably conceived and there is a dramatic reality about the group which vividly recalls the incident it so well portrays.

As you look down the garden, with the laundry to the left and the wood to the right, you call to mind that it was before this low building that the mysterious vision of her father passed to lose itself amidst the trees, a vision which made such an indelible impression on her mind, the significance of which she was to know only too well in later years.

Beside this laundry our beloved Saint had her little garden; in one of the laundry windows may be seen one of those little altars she loved to make, and then run eagerly to call her father to come and see it. To please her he would appear lost in admiration at her masterpiece; and, indeed, faded as it is now, we recognize that it was indeed fashioned by the hand of a true artist.

Here everything speaks to us of that marvellous family life, so united by the bonds of love, both natural and supernatural, which make it an enduring model for all Christian families, for today and all the days to come. Here we have set before us in its quiet dignity the Christian home in which love reigns supreme, where there is no feverish rush after the fleeting pleasures of earth, but the quiet, ordered round of life in which God is all in all.

The next point of pilgrimage is the Benedictine Convent of her school days, her Confirmation and First Communion. Starting again from the Carmelite Convent, you turn again to the right and then take the first turning to the left, the Boulevard St. Anne, along which you continue till you reach the rue Gustave David on your left. A short distance down on your left you will find the Church of St. Désir, an interesting example of Renaissance work; note particularly on the Gospel side of the choir the remarkably powerful group of the Madonna and Child, a very fine work indeed.

Coming out of the Church and continuing still to the left a few steps bring you to the Convent. This is a late Renaissance building, solid and serious, such as befits the home of nuns of the venerable Benedictine Order. The convent church remains exactly as it was when St. Thérèse knew it. There at that grille

197

she made her First Communion, for she and her companions were inside the Convent and made their Communion at the same grille as the nuns. Here, too, is the Missal on which she placed her hands on that memorable afternoon when she read the Act of Consecration to the Blessed Virgin in the name of all the first communicants. The nun who was her class-mistress is still living. You see also the place where the religious instructions were given, and where the Children of Mary met, and many little souvenirs of her connection with the Convent.

Next you visit the magnificent thirteenth-century cathedral of St. Pierre; it was in the marvellously beautiful fifteenth-century Lady Chapel behind the choir that St. Thérèse used to hear Mass and receive Holy Communion. And in the Chapel on the Gospel side of the choir, St. Thérèse and her father used to assist at solemn Mass and Vespers on Sunday.

The next visit will, of course, be to the magnificent Basilica which I have already described in the previous chapter. In order to reach it, always starting from the Carmelite Church, turn to the right, then very sharply to the right again and then a few paces further down on the left you will see the road leading to the Basilica. Besides the Basilica you will, of course, visit the very monumental Way of the Cross which was dedicated on the last day of the Holy Year in honour of the nineteenth centenary of our Redemption.

This Way of the Cross, surmounted by a magnificent Calvary, stands on the high ground behind the Basilica. A wall, surmounted by a simple balustrade of columns without capitals, with pilasters at intervals supporting life-size figures of angels holding emblems of the Passion, marks the beginning of the Way of the Cross. These figures are a very fine example of the sculptor's art, life-size and of admirable simplicity. In the centre of this retaining wall, in an arched recess, is the first

198

station, above which is a simple Cross in relief against a gabled canopy. On both sides a flight of steps leads up to the first level, where, on either side of a vast space, three stations are placed in arched recesses of fine architectural setting, joined together by columns supporting the architrave which unites the whole, while the pylons at each end are surmounted by bronze lamps to give light at night.

A word must be said as to the treatment of the stations themselves. They are of stone in high relief, and give the impression that the spectator is looking at various incidents through an opening; hence the figures are generally three-quarter length, and wisely, too, the sculptor has limited the number of his figures in each station. To avoid the necessity of the pilgrims retracing their steps, the second, third and fourth stations are on the right, and fifth, sixth and seventh on the left of this first terrace.

A central flight of steps leads up to the second terrace, where the same arrangement is followed: the eighth, ninth and tenth stations being on the right, and the eleventh, twelfth and thirteenth on the left.

This second terrace is closed by the great Calvary with an open colonnade on either side. The great Cross on which the majestic figure of Christ is sculptured is a remarkably vigorous piece of work. Just below the Cross is a great arched recess in which is an altar for saying Mass in the open, reached by a flight of steps on either side of the Calvary. Between these flights of steps, another flight leads down to the Sepulchre, the fourteenth station. Before this second terrace, on great pilasters, are four angels holding the emblems of Christ's Royalty and Divinity. The ornament is in low relief wrought in a similar manner to that of ancient Celtic work. On these two terraces a vast multitude can hear Mass on the occasion of those great gatherings when the church would be too small to contain them.

Lastly there is the cemetery. You follow the same road as for the Basilica, but instead of turning off, you continue straight on, and after about fifteen minutes walk you reach the entrance. Without much difficulty you find the little section which belongs to the Carmelites. On the exact spot where the body of our little Mistress was buried a fine stone statue stands, the work of Dom Marie-Bernard. Here in these lovely surroundings, for the cemetery is situated on the side of a hill, with the wooded hills on the other side of the valley, the birds singing and the sun shining, St. Thérèse seems extraordinarily near. It was just such a widespread landscape as this which she loved.

But the whole city of Lisieux speaks of our little Mistress, for it was along these very Boulevards with their trees, through these streets with their charming medieval houses, in the park with its magnificent trees that, in company with her father and sisters, she passed so frequently, less than forty-seven years ago. And Lisieux itself has changed extraordinarily little since her time. The hermitage for women and girl pilgrims and the Maison St. Jean for priest pilgrims have arisen in the rue de Carmel, and one or two new hotels to meet the needs of the ever-increasing stream of pilgrims are the only outward signs of change we see.

All the time we are in Lisieux we feel in an extraordinary degree in the company of our little Saint. Certainly I would say to every one of her disciples try and spend at least a few days of quiet and recollection in company with her in her own city of Lisieux. You will come away with renewed courage to face all the struggles and difficulties of life in these difficult days. She will be favourable to you at Lisieux.

CHAPTER XX
ST. THÉRÈSE AND THE NEW AGE

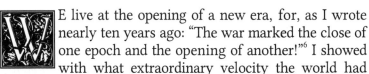

E live at the opening of a new era, for, as I wrote nearly ten years ago: "The war marked the close of one epoch and the opening of another!"[6] I showed with what extraordinary velocity the world had moved forward during those four fateful years, and it has moved no less swiftly since, as anyone will perceive who looks back over the past sixteen years. Does this accelerated movement mean that the world hastens to the final consummation? That would appear to be the thought of the reigning Pontiff, for in his address preceding the Beatification of our little Teacher he said: "Today in a few hours is accomplished that which formerly demanded years, and in a few years that which formerly required centuries. The world speeds along with vertiginous velocity, and from the rapidity of its course—*motus in fine velocior*—one may conclude that it hastens towards the end."[7]

"Watchman, what of the night?" What is this new age like upon which we have entered? In many ways not unlike the pagan world which the first Christians had to face, for the world-spirit remains the same through the ages. As St.

---

[6] *The Real Thing*. Kegan Paul, Trench, Trübner & co.

[7] *Story of the Canonization of St. Thérèse of Lisieux*, p. 89. Burns Oates & Washbourne.

Augustine has shown in his immortal work *The City of God,* there have been from the beginning two kingdoms: the Kingdom of God and the Kingdom of the Devil.

The warning of the apostle of Love in the first century is equally necessary now: "Love not the world, neither the things that are in the world ... all that is in the world, the lust of the flesh, the lust of the eyes and the pride of life is not of the Father, but of the world."

But the flood of neo-paganism which has swept over the world, sometimes differing in outward manifestation it is true, but always one in essence, has this difference. The old pagan world had some moral principles, the neo-pagan world has none, for it has neither the morality of Christianity nor that of ancient paganism.

It denies the whole of Christian morality, defies all the safeguards which Christian modesty has guarded so jealously through the ages, and claims unrestrained licence for all the disordered passions of humanity as the only law. What we call good, it calls evil; what we call light, it calls darkness. Hence the contrast between these two kingdoms could not be more complete than it is, and the words of St. John are more than ever verified: "The whole world lieth in the arms of the wicked one." There is significance in these words, for it means that the world lies willingly, unresistingly in the arms of the Devil, quite content to be there, quite content with what he has to offer.

The Holy Father, in his great Encyclical *Casti Connubi,* said: "The most pernicious errors and depraved morals have begun to spread even amongst the faithful. ... Now, no longer secretly, or under cover, but openly, with all sense of shame put aside, by word and by writing, by theatrical representations of every kind, by fiction, by amorous and frivolous novels, by cinemas picturing in vivid scenes, by radio, in short, by all the inventions of modern science the sanctity of marriage is trampled under foot and derided; divorce, adultery, all the basest vices are extolled or depicted in such guise as to appear free of all reproach and infamy." And he goes on to show how widespread is the evil: These ideas are instilled into people of every class, rich and poor, master and man, lettered and unlettered, married and single, godly and godless, old and young, and alas, for these last, as easiest prey, the worst snares are spread."

Here is a picture of the neo-paganism which we have to fight, for with it there can be no compromise; but only a fight to the death. And to battle with this neo-pagan world, so swelling with pride and overweening arrogance, which throws down the challenge like Goliath of old, God has in these last days given us a leader in the young Virgin of Lisieux who comes to oppose to the pride and lust of paganism her doctrine of true humility, pure chastity, holy simplicity and perfect love. "I burn," she exclaims, "to battle for Your glory. ... *My sword is Love.* With it I shall drive the invader from the kingdom and have You proclaimed King of Souls." God has given His sure promise: "*When the enemy shall come in like a flood, the Lord shall lift up a standard against him.*" And that standard is St. Thérèse of Lisieux, for God will once again manifest His power in weakness and bring to nought the Pride of Hell by means of the humility of His humble Handmaiden, for "the foolishness of God is wiser than men and the weakness of God is stronger than men."

As we look at the kingdom of this Darkness, seemingly so mighty and overwhelming in its strength and assured confidence, we may be inclined to feel how inadequate for the task is the one God has chosen, as inadequate as was David to face Goliath or the first Christians to affront the might of the greatest Empire the world has ever seen. Goliath was slain, the Roman Empire perished; but the Church of God remains.

The triumphs of the world are palpable, visible to the senses; the triumphs of Grace hidden and secret: "The things which are seen are temporal, the things which are not seen are eternal." When God made choice of our little Mistress as our Teacher and Leader for these last days, He sent her to the Cloisters of Carmel where she would to outward seeming be hidden completely and for ever. Yet her apostolate has embraced the world. And this apostolate has progressed almost as secretly as her life. What does the Press, what does the world know of it? Yet it is the most outstanding fact of our times. Her complete writings, which, as she knew, were destined to be the chief weapon of her apostolate, have in the French edition alone exceeded three-quarters of a million, while the smaller edition has run to two and a half millions, and *Novissima Verba* (containing the account of her last days), has reached a circulation of 110,000. This is for France alone, and the circulation of the English, Italian and Spanish editions have been at least as numerous. Altogether her works have been translated into more than thirty-three languages.

Millions all the world over have been inspired by her words to follow her *little way*, which more than once since her death she has declared to be so safe and sure. New religious congregations under her patronage have arisen in Europe, America, Asia and Africa; miracles of healing surpassing those of any other saint have attested the truth of her teaching, for the Lord has been with her, confirming her words by miracles and signs following. "Universality is one of the characteristics of sanctity,' writes M. Albert de Pouvourville,[8] "we may well think it was the enthusiasm of the world towards her which led the Ecclesiastical Authorities to relax the rule of the delay of fifty years which had hitherto been observed so rigorously." Speaking of her universal action in the Great War, he says: "It was enough for any human being to turn to her . . . here it is a Frenchman; there an Englishman, or Roumanian, or again, a German." The Great War increased both the glory and the followers of Thérèse, just in proportion to the degree in which it increased the anguish of the world. In the presence of that universal catastrophe she passed the frontiers of her province and her country. The rush of enthusiasm which carried men to the feet of the Carmelite is unique in the history of the Christian Faith."

The world in its might is arrayed against us, we face it unafraid, for, like our beloved little Leader, we are soldiers as well as lovers. We fight because we love, and, like our little Mistress, we are ready to do battle till we die.

No surrender, no compromise with error. Never under cover of a false charity will we compromise or modify the truth *even if by so doing we could reconcile to the Church all the heretics in the world.*

No surrender where faith or morality are at stake, whether proximately or remotely. We must be faithful to Christian modesty in our words, our dress and our conduct. Remember how the Christian virgins of long ago, when tossed by wild beasts in the arena, with their dying hands rearranged their disordered vesture that so even in that supreme moment they might not appear lacking in modesty.

Look at St. Melania, a Roman Virgin of the last days of the

---

[8] *Sainte Thérèse de Lisieux, Protectrice des peuples.* Editions du Lys. Paris.

fourth century, heiress to fabulous wealth, allied by birth to the Imperial family, she renounced it all, cast aside her splendid raiment, and even when she appeared in the Emperor's presence would not lay aside her simple veil and dress of wool. That was in the dying days of the Empire when, as now, painted faces, extravagant dress and contempt for morality heralded the coming doom. St. Melania and those like her faced the dying pagan world with unfaltering courage, and we must face our neo-pagan world with a courage not less than theirs.

A favourite text of our little Mistress which was often upon her lips, we may well make our own: "Do manfully and your heart shall be strengthened," and she used to say that if we boldly take the first step we shall perceive the presence of God's strength to help us.

It is this first step which costs most as well as counts most. Once we have taken it boldly and courageously the rest is easy. To try and serve God and the world at the same time is the most miserable of compromises, and they who try to do so are much to be pitied, for they have neither the enduring satisfaction of the Faith nor the fleeting satisfaction of the world. A religion of compromise will never inspire anybody, youth least of all.

The Catholic Religion demands sacrifice because it is real, and sacrifice appeals as it has ever done to all that is best in human kind. A religion which reduced its demands to a minimum, calls for no sacrifice and is only intent on showing how easily the kingdoms of this world and the next can be combined, will excite no enthusiasm, since it calls for no sacrifice.

ST. THÉRÈSE AND THE NEW AGE

No, we must be the real thing, out and out Catholics, and as a consequence renounce much which others may enjoy. We must abstain from being present at representations, whether at the theatre or the cinema, which assail Christian morality and modesty. The Holy Father has referred in no uncertain terms to the havoc wrought by the latter: "For some time past we have been receiving detailed reports from Cardinals, Archbishops and Bishops in every part of the world which show how widespread is this evil. All without exception deplore in the strongest terms the disastrous influence of the cinema." Abstinence is a sure remedy, for if all those who are on the side of morality stay away, the protest of vacant seats will produce more effect on those responsible than the most eloquent words. By staying away we shall preserve our own soul from harm and also the souls of others who might be led into danger by our example.

The Disciples of St. Thérèse are very specially bound to do their part in this fight against the Kingdom of Darkness, they must be foremost in the fight, and give no place to the Devil. On earth we are soldiers until our last breath, and we must never forget it. In Heaven we shall be Lovers alone, and soldiers no more, because the war will be over. Then in the Light of that day, all the struggle and suffering of earth will appear as nothing in comparison with the joy and the glory that are ours.

St. Thérèse, our holy little Leader, arm us for the fight, let us feel your presence in the day of battle. You have promised to "come down," fulfil your promise, and when the fight is fiercest come to our aid. Keep us true to Jesus, our Adorable King, may we exist for Him alone, live in His Will, desire nought but His pleasure and for His Love trample under foot all the temptations of the flesh, all the seductions of the world, all the snares of the Devil, and may we hear Him saying at the last: "Well done, good and faithful servant, enter thou into the joy of Thy Lord." Amen! Amen! Amen!

THE END

Other Books you may like from Mediatrix Press:

The Life of the Venerable Anne of Jesus, OCD
A Sister of Notre Dame de Namur

The History of St. Norbert: Apostle of the Eucharist
Cornelius Kirkfleet

The Life of St. Francis of Assisi
Candide Chalippe, OFM

The Franciscan way of the Cross
In a new translation

The Spiritual Life of Cardinal Merry del Val
Jerome de Gal

A Champion of the Church: The Life of St. Peter Canisius
by William Reany

The Autobiography of St. Charles of Sezze
St. Charles of Sezze

The Public Life of Our Lord Jesus Christ
Alban Goodier, S.J.

The Life of St. Philip Neri
Anne Hope

St. John Fisher: Reformer, Humanist, Martyr
E.E. Reynolds

St. Thomas More: A Great Man in Hard Times
E.E. Reynolds

For more information on these and other titles, visit
Mediatrix Press online, at: www.mediatrixpress.com

211